Samuel Hemphill

The Diatessaron of Tatian

A Harmony of the Four Gospels Compiled in the Third Quarter of the

Second Century   .

Samuel Hemphill

The Diatessaron of Tatian
A Harmony of the Four Gospels Compiled in the Third Quarter of the Second Century

ISBN/EAN: 9783337279745

Printed in Europe, USA, Canada, Australia, Japan

Cover: Foto ©Lupo / pixelio.de

More available books at **www.hansebooks.com**

THE
DIATESSARON OF TATIAN

A HARMONY OF THE FOUR HOLY GOSPELS COMPILED
IN THE THIRD QUARTER OF THE
SECOND CENTURY;

NOW FIRST EDITED IN AN ENGLISH FORM

WITH

INTRODUCTION AND APPENDICES.

BY THE

REV. SAMUEL HEMPHILL, B.D.,
PROFESSOR OF BIBLICAL GREEK IN THE UNIVERSITY OF DUBLIN.

LONDON:
HODDER & STOUGHTON,
27 PATERNOSTER ROW.

DUBLIN:
WILLIAM McGEE,
18 NASSAU STREET.

1888.

Entered at Stationers' Hall.]

PRINTED BY
SEALY, BRYERS AND WALKER,
MIDDLE ABBEY STREET,
DUBLIN.

TO MY FATHER,

ROBERT HEMPHILL,

OF

SPRINGHILL, IN THE COUNTY TIPPERARY:

A MEMBER OF THE GENERAL SYNOD

OF THE CHURCH OF IRELAND

EVER SINCE ITS FIRST SESSION:

A SUPPORTER OF THE CAUSE OF THE ORPHAN

A RELIABLE FRIEND:

AND

A GOOD FATHER.

PREFACE.

THE materials of a patchwork must exist before the patchwork itself. The shells and pebbles which we find embedded in the matrix of a conglomerate rock, must first have had a separate existence grinding themselves smooth on the troubled sea-shore. So it is but a truism to say, that the records which Tatian knew and valued as *the* authentic form of apostolic tradition, and from which he compiled his Harmony, must have had an assured position in his time. He knew—at any rate he used—no others. And he was the friend and pupil of Justin Martyr. They lived and taught in the same city ; were received in the same circle of acquaintances ; were persecuted by the same enemies ; worshipped—perhaps hid—in the same catacombs. And when the friends wanted to strengthen or comfort one another, in the face of danger or difficulty, we may well believe that they quoted the Saviour's words, and recounted His deeds, out of the same Gospels.

But to admit that the Gospels of Tatian were the Gospels of Justin, is to bring them back to the very threshold of the first century, to a period in which very many personal friends of the apostles must have been alive, and able to testify to the genuineness of their writings.

It has been an ever-increasing pleasure to me to work at this little book : and, though keenly sensible of its faults and failings, still I cannot but take a certain pride in it, as

b

the first edition in which the earliest Harmony of the Gospels has become accessible in any form to the English student.

I have most thankfully to express my obligations to Dr. Salmon, Provost of Trinity College, and to Dr. Gwynn, Regius Professor of Divinity in the University of Dublin, for their unfailing kindness in helping and encouraging me at various times during my study of the subject. Dr. Stokes, Professor of Ecclesiastical History, has also shown most genuine sympathy and interest in the work. While among my contemporaries, I have to acknowledge valuable help from the Rev. William Colgan, and the Rev. H. Jackson Lawlor, B.D. ; to the latter of whom it is due to say, that his kind and acute criticisms have contributed to make the book less unworthy of consideration by competent judges.

S. H.

TRINITY COLLEGE, DUBLIN,
    19th October, 1888.

CONTENTS.

———+———

INTRODUCTION.

———

I. THE MAN TATIAN.

THE City of Rome—the Eternal City, as it is called—has witnessed many a strange revolution of the wheel of Fortune.

This very year a book has there issued from the press, which well illustrates the truth of this remark. It is an Arabic work of the tenth century, a translation of a lost Syriac original; and it bears on its title page the famous name of "*Tatian's Harmony of the Gospels*,"[1] while its inscription is to Pope Leo XIII. as the choicest offering which the Scribes of the Vatican library could contribute towards the recent celebration of his Jubilee.

Yet, seventeen centuries ago, what heartburnings the very mention of that same Tatian would have caused in the Church of Rome! And how many painful incidents could the elder Christians of that city have then recounted, of the controversies which had raged round his person some score of years before, and which had led to his withdrawal from among them, branded with the stigma of heresy, and mayhap denounced by the then Pope as a foe to Christianity!

Now, it would be hazardous to assert that these early Roman Churchmen were wrong in the verdict which, informally at least, they pronounced upon the opinions and teaching of Tatian.

---

[1] Tatiani Evangeliorum Harmoniae Arabice nunc primum ex duplici codice edidit et translatione Latina donavit P. Augustinus Ciasca, &c. Romae, 1888.

We have at present no means of knowing the exact nature of that verdict, still less the grounds on which it rested.

That Tatian held strange and even heretical notions about the spirit-world; unworthy conceptions of the Creator; and unholy and debased views of marriage, must be conceded[1], and from all that we can learn about the natural temper and disposition of the man, they would probably lead him to expound and enforce these with extraordinary warmth and even bitterness,[2] to the great detriment of concord, and the consequent weakening of the Church. Still, as we have to depend on the statements of adversaries only, the greater part of his own voluminous writings[3] having perished, we are surely justified in thinking that popular prejudice, then as now, may have had a large share in the preparation of the hated roll of heretics; and that Tatian was far from being as black as he was painted in the controversial treatises of a later age.

Allowance must also be made for one whose life was so chequered.

Born early in the second century in the far East; trained not only in his native Syriac, but in the philosophy and polite literature of the Greeks; filled, while yet a boy, with an insatiable thirst for knowledge; a traveller, like Mahomet, through many countries in search of truth; initiated into the inner mysteries of the heathen cults; and then at last when weary and heart-sick with the cruelty, immorality and dishonesty of paganism, captivated and entranced by the simple charm of the Sacred Scriptures—the barbaric letters— upon which by a Divine chance he one day lighted.

We next find him at Rome an ardent convert, and a pupil

---

[1] For the allusions to Tatian's life and opinions see Iren. i. 28. 1. and iii. 23. 8. Rhodon in Euseb. H.E. v. 13 : Clem. Al. Strom. iii. 12 : Euseb. H.E. iv. 29 : Epiph. Haer. 46. 1 : Jerome de vir. il. 29., Praef. in Com. in Tit., adv. Jovin. i. 3 : Theodoret Haer. Fab. i. 20 : besides what Tatian says of himself in his Oratio contra Graecos chaps. 29, 35, 42.

[2] See *Oratio* Chaps. 2, 3, 8, 10, 14, &c., for his methods of controversy against the heathen.

[3] Eusebius. H.E. iv. 29, says that he left a great multitude of writings; and alludes to his work on the Pauline epp. Rhodon *l.c.* mentions his work on problems connected with the hidden and obscure things of the sacred writings. Clement *l.c.* mentions a work by him on Christian perfection : and the *Oratio* itself mentions a zoological treatise by its author. Chap. 15.

of the sainted Justin, whose martyrdom he very nearly shared. Like Justin also, he gave public instruction in Christianity, and wrote a powerful and most interesting Apology, the only work of his which has hitherto been recognized as extant.[1]

It is from the autobiographical portion of this Apology that we glean what little we know of his early life and conversion[2]; but incidentally also from its abrupt, incisive, and unusual tone, we are able to gather much about the character of the writer.[3]

Unlike the broad and philosophic Justin, Tatian flings from him every vestige of respect for Greek literature and culture. His "*Apology*" is one sarcastic exposure of the weakness and wickedness of heathenism. The vials of his irony and anger are poured forth to such an extent that we insensibly think of him as a man of audacious, uncompromising, and peculiar mind, neither caring for the feelings, nor respecting the traditions of those from whom he had for ever separated ; and whom he had come to regard with a scorn which sought no disguise.

Now the suspicion is irresistible that the bitterness and narrowness with which he thus attacked paganism in his Apology, may in later years have sprung up afresh and widened the breach which his unusual opinions were already causing in the Roman Church. At any rate he left Rome, as I have said, smarting under the accusation of heresy, and being made to feel that his influence for good had outlived itself; and after perhaps many wanderings, at last settled down in his native Mesopotamia,[4] where his "*views*" would create no alarm, and where he could feel perfectly free to preach the blessed Gospel after his own notions to his still unevangelized countrymen. What a lesson for persons who nowadays strike out separate paths for themselves in religion, and shrink not from sowing disunion, and rending the Body of Christ at home, while the hundreds of millions of heathen lie open before them, stretching out their hands in vain, and crying bitterly for teachers.

Of Tatian's last years we are left entirely to conjecture, nor can we be certain of either the place or the date of his

---

[1] The best ed. of the *Oratio* is Otto. *Corpus Apologetarum, &c. Vol. vi.* Jena. 1851.
[2] Especially chapters 29, 35, 42.
[3] See Prof. Fuller, Art. TATIAN, *Encyc. Brit.*, 1887.
[4] Epiph. *l.c.*

death.[1] But this we do know, that his name never recovered
its popularity at Rome, or in the Greek and Latin Churches
generally, where for many centuries he was viewed with
that peculiar dislike and distrust which inevitably gather
round a man on whom public opinion has once imprinted
its ominous brand of "heretic."

Such then is an outline of Tatian's life: the Christian
portion of which is thus seen to resolve itself into two
distinct periods, the Roman or Western, in which he
lectured and wrote in behalf of Christianity, and attained
unpleasant notoriety as a heretic; and the Syrian or Eastern,
in which he probably spent the rest of his days preaching
the gospel on the banks of the Euphrates.

II. THE DIATESSARON IN THE EARLY CHURCH.

WE have seen Tatian as a teacher at Rome, and have
followed him into the obscurity of his Eastern retirement.
Let us now pass to consider his Diatessaron, or so-called
Harmony[2] of the Four Gospels; and let us at once face the
question, why so little has been hitherto known of it. The
answer is simply this, that the Diatessaron has been sought
where it did not exist, and therefore could not be found. It
has been tacitly assumed, because Tatian taught at Rome,
wrote his other works in Greek, (which was the usual
language at Rome in his day), and gave a Greek name to
his compilation of the Gospels, that therefore it was written
in Greek, and belonged in a manner to the western sphere
of its author's labours. Yet, from the whole body of western
Christian literature which we have before us, it is scarcely
possible to glean any allusion at all to the Diatessaron
before the middle of the sixth century, when Victor, Bishop
of Capua, found an anonymous Latin Gospel-Harmony and

---

[1] It is indeed generally believed that he died in the neighbourhood
of Edessa, about A.D. 180. For the chronology of Tatian's later years
see Zahn. *Tatian's Diatessaron* Erlangen 1881, pp. 276-292: Lightfoot
Art. in *Contemporary Review*, May, 1877, p. 1133. For general
information about his life see Articles by Dr. Wace in *Expositor* 1881
and 1882; Professor Fuller's Art. *Tatian* in Smith's Dict. of Christian
Biog., 1887; and Professor Harnack's Art. *Tatian* in Encyc. Brit. 1888.

[2] It was not a Harmony in the modern sense of the word, but a kind
of patchwork Gospel. Its principle was *amalgamation* not *comparison*;
to use the words of Lightfoot.

inferred that it must be the work of Tatian.[1] Let us divide early Christian literature into Latin, Greek, and Syriac, and see what is the conclusion to be drawn from the evidence of each group as to the sphere where the Diatessaron exercised its influence.

First as to Latin literature. Not only is there no mention of the Diatessaron in any Latin author before the middle of the sixth century, but we can go so far as to say that Latin Christianity could have known nothing about it before that date. Several Latin writers can be mentioned, who could not have failed to have known and noticed the book, if it had existed in Latin in their day.[2]

Victor of Capua himself is an important witness; for he was skilled in both Greek and Latin, and was a man of considerable eminence as a scholar and controversialist.[3] And his solitary reason for attributing his discovery to Tatian, is that he found one passage in Eusebius which spoke of Tatian having compiled a patchwork Gospel,[4] which he judged to be the same, substantially, as that which accidentally came into his own hands. Not one other allusion to Tatian's work does Victor mention; and the conclusion is, that, but for the statement of Eusebius, he would have remained perfectly ignorant that such a work had ever existed.

Again, Cassiodorus, who was a contemporary of Victor, says nothing about such a work in his *Instituta Divina*. Neither does Gelasius include it in his *Decretum de recipiendis et non recipiendis libris*. Jerome is silent as to any Latin version of it in his strictures on the great multiplication of Latin bibles. So is Augustine in his treatise, *De consensu Evangelistarum*. Nor, finally, is there any allusion to the book in the poet Juvencus, who (A.D. 330) wrote a poetical Gospel History, and had to construct a Harmony for himself.[5]

---

[1] See the work and Victor's preface in Migne Pat. Lat., vol. 68, or Ranke's edition of the Codex Fuldensis, 1868.

[2] Much of the following is a reproduction of the reasoning of Zahn. Part I.

[3] His "most celebrated work was that on the Paschal Cycle mentioned by several chroniclers and praised by Bede."—Smith's Dict. of Xn. Biog. Art. *Victor*.

[4] Euseb. H. E. iv. 29. ὁ Τατιανὸς συνάφειάν τινα καὶ συναγωγὴν οὐκ οἶδ' ὅπως τῶν εὐαγγελίων συνθείς, τὸ Διὰ τεσσάρων τοῦτο προσωνόμασεν. ὃ καὶ παρά τισιν εἰσέτι νῦν φέρεται.

[5] Pat. Lat. vol. xix., p. 52.

We conclude then that the book exercised no influence on Latin Christianity before the time of Victor ; but that it would have exercised great influence if it had existed in Latin is evident from the experience of the ninth and following centuries, as will afterwards be shown ;[1] therefore it did not exist in Latin, nor did the early Latin Church know anything whatever about it.

Let us now glance at Greek Christian literature. Its whole range supplies us with but three references to the Diatessaron. Before we discuss these separately, let us not fail to remark how strange it is that so little influence should have been exercised on Greek Christianity by a Gospel-Harmony, compiled by the author of the celebrated Apology, the friend and companion of Justin Martyr. Judged by the *e silentio* argument, the Greeks were about as ignorant as the Latins of the nature, or even the existence of the Diatessaron.

Irenaeus, who held such very strict notions about the necessity of the fourfold narrative,[2] and who would have been shocked at the bare mention of a patchwork Gospel, such as Victor of Capua had found described in Eusebius, though he twice[3] controverts Tatian's opinions, says not one word of his Diatessaron. It is scarcely possible then to conceive that he had ever heard of the book.

In the last chapter of the fifth book of the History of Eusebius, there are several extensive quotations from an author who has been supposed to be Hippolytus. Now two things may be distinctly proved from the way in which Tatian's name occurs in these extracts. The first of these is that the author could not have been Hippolytus ; for Hippolytus speaks with disfavour of Tatian, and mentions his heresy, whereas the extracts place Tatian's name in the honourable company of Justin, Miltiades, Clement, and many others, who wrote against the heathen on behalf of the truth, and who controverted the heresies of their day. Photius says that the author of these extracts was Caius, and Dr. Salmon[4] strongly inclines to this view. But the second point is of greater importance in the present enquiry. It is this :—that the author mentions the fact that the followers of Artemon had shamelessly tampered with Scripture,[5] yet

---

[1] See Appendix D.
[2] Salmon. Introduction to the N.T. pp. 38-9.
[3] i. 28. 1 and iii. 23. 8.
[4] Introduction to the N.T. p. 55.
[5] γραφὰς μὲν θείας ἀφόβως ῥεραδιουργήκασι.

quotes Tatian as a defender of the faith, thereby proving that he had never heard that he acted in a similar manner.

But let us get a little closer to the man himself : let us enter the company of those who had personally known him in his better days, and we shall find that though they resented the errors into which he drifted, they never knew of his treatment of the Gospel.

Rhodon, of Asia Minor, undertook to refute his master's work on the difficulties and contradictions of the Old Testament,[1] yet we never read that he knew of the work in which he sought to present the Evangelical narratives in a form free from difficulties and seeming contradictions. Clement of Alexandria, also a supposed pupil of Tatian,[2] makes several allusions to his heretical views,[3] but preserves an impenetrable silence as to the Diatessaron. So then we have four men of his time, who were intimate with his writings and opinions, and yet never heard of his Gospel-Harmony. The conclusion is that it was not a book which, at first at any rate, exercised much influence on Greek Christianity. But that it did not exercise much influence at a later date is evident from the witness of Hesychius of Jerusalem, more than two centuries later ;[4] for he says that anyone *could* make a Harmony of all the history,[5] but he never mentions one as having been already made ; which is tolerably clear proof that he had never heard of the Diatessaron.

Let us now consider the three passages of Greek literature which mention the Diatessaron. They are passages of Eusebius (*see above*), Epiphanius, and Theodoret. And, so far as their evidence is concerned, the conclusion is only confirmed, that the influence of the Diatessaron on Greek Christianity was *nil.* Theodoret though he wrote his work on Heresies in Greek, was the Bishop of a Syrian diocese, and must be taken as representing Syrian not Greek Christianity. Epiphanius spoke Syriac as his native language, and is

---

[1] Euseb. H.E. v. 13.
[2] Strom. i. 1. where he mentions that one of his teachers was "an Assyrian." cf. Oratio ch. 1.
[3] Strom. iii. 12.
[4] He was called "the Theologian," see Smith's D.C.B.
[5] In Dom. res., Combefis, Auct. nov. i. 765, D. ὥστε δύνασθαί τινα κατὰ τὴν τῶν καιρῶν τάξιν τὰ παρ' ἑκάστου γεγραμμένα συνθέντα μίαν ἁρμονίαν κ. ἓν σῶμα πάσης τῆς ἱστορίας ἐργάσασθαι, καθάπερ ἑνὸς τὸ πᾶν γεγραφότος κ. οὐ πολλῶν.
Zahn. p. 31, note 1, misquotes, πάσης ἱστορίας.

therefore not a pure representative of Western ideas and knowledge. And Eusebius was a man of such wide acquaintance with the history and literature of both the East and West (though probably not a good Syriac scholar), that the fact of his knowing a work would not prove that it was generally known by other Greeks of his day.

We shall, however, take Eusebius and Epiphanius as fair representatives of Greek Church literature, and examine their evidence as to the Diatessaron. Eusebius says :—

"Tatian composed a sort of connexion and compilation,[1] I know not how, of the Gospels : and called it τὸ διὰ τεσσάρων. This work is current in some quarters even to the present day."

Now Zahn and other good critics regard it as certain from these words that Eusebius himself had never seen the Diatessaron. He calls it *a sort of* connexion and compilation of the Gospels, and he vaguely states that this work is current *in some quarters,* (or among some persons), even to the present day ; giving us no hint as to *where* it was current, *the kind of persons* who used it, or the *language* in which it was written. Again consider the confession of ignorance which seems to be contained in the phrase, "I know not how" (οὐκ οἶδ' ὅπως). It is, indeed, true that so high an authority as Bishop Lightfoot urges that this expression in idiomatic English signifies "I cannot think what he was about," and is equivalent to "unaccountably," "absurdly ;" so that, if anything, it implies knowledge rather than ignorance of the contents.[2] In support of this contention, Lightfoot quotes twenty-six examples of the use of the phrase in Origen's work against Celsus ; and lays stress on the fact that Origen had the work of Celsus before him, and sometimes actually uses the expression of the very passage on which he is commenting. Still it cannot be denied that the combination οὐκ οἶδ' ὅπως is found in Classical Greek to express *ignorance,*[3] and therefore it is hard to see why Eusebius may not have chosen to employ it in that sense. Besides, as Zahn very forcibly points out, Eusebius, great a literary critic as he was, has given no description whatever of the plan or principle of Tatian's work, not even in the way of disparagement ; whereas he has expressed his approval of

---

[1] H. E. iv. 29, Lightfoot's translations are mainly followed as given in *Cont. Rev.*
συνάφειάν τινα καὶ συναγωγὴν.............συνθείς.
[2] *l. c*, p. 1136.   [3] Sophocles, O.T. 1367.

the somewhat kindred work of Ammonius, which he knew well.[1] The truth seems to be, that Eusebius knew the book only by hearsay, and being well aware that its author was a heretic, took it for granted that his compilation was a mere distorted Gospel, like that of Marcion and the other Gnostic teachers. At any rate, we know that Eusebius knew of Tatian's work on the Pauline Epistles, and his Problems, only through hearsay : and his description of the Diatessaron is just what might be expected from one who had the same kind of vague information about it. This being the first attempt of the kind, Eusebius would have nothing to guide him in forming an opinion ; nor could he or any other orthodox writer easily believe that Holy Scripture would have been subjected to such violent treatment except for heretical purposes ; and having once made up his mind that the book was a sort of heretical Gospel, we may well believe that he would take no great trouble to procure and examine it for himself.

Let us pass on to Epiphanius. His words are :—[2]

"The Diatessaron Gospel is said to have been composed by him (Tatian). It is called by some the Gospel according to the Hebrews."

Now these words puzzled critics very much for a long time ; nor was there any ready way of explaining them, except by supposing that Epiphanius here, as in so many other places, made a blunder.[3] But we must be fair even to Epiphanius. He says, "It is called *by some* the Gospel according to the Hebrews," but as Zahn notices, he himself does not call it so ; and, moreover, whenever he alludes to the Gospel according to the Hebrews, he does so quite apart from any reference to Tatian. His view of the Hebrew Gospel is that it is a mangled edition of S. Matthew ; so that here he merely chronicles the mistake of other persons. Does not this distinctly prove that Epiphanius had never seen the Diatessaron ? And does it not also prove that his informants could have had but a very superficial knowledge of it ? The fact is, that the Diatessaron, as we shall presently see, was current in Syriac, and was known to be the work of a heretic ; at the same time, and in an adjoining tract of country,[4] the Hebrew Gospel was used by the heretical Nazarenes ; and certain Greek-speaking people meeting the two works in about the same locality, hearing of the heretical authorship

---

[1] Letter to Carpianus. This argument is strengthened by the discovery that S. Mat. was the basis of both.
[2] Haer. 46, 1   [3] Lightfoot.   [4] Beraea, the modern Aleppo.

of each, and noticing that both were written in oriental characters, which they could not read, hastily concluded that they were one and the same work, and so reported to Epiphanius.

So far therefore as early non-Syrian Christianity is concerned, we may safely say that the Diatessaron exercised practically no influence before the sixth century : and even the little that we do read of it in Eusebius and Epiphanius confirms the conclusion that it could not have belonged to that portion of Tatian's life in which he flourished at Rome, but to that later portion in which he laboured among his Syrian fellow-countrymen.

At any rate history begins to find her voice the moment we touch Syrian soil : and we there find the Diatessaron "at home." Take Theodoret for example, the Bishop of Cyrrhus near the Euphrates. In the year 453 he wrote the following words :—[1]

"He (Tatian) composed the Gospel which is called *Diatessaron*, cutting out the genealogies and such other passages as show the Lord to have been born of the seed of David after the flesh. This work was in use not only among persons belonging to his sect, but also among those who follow the apostolic doctrine, as they did not perceive the mischief of the composition, but used the book in all simplicity on account of its brevity. And I myself found more than two hundred such copies held in respect in the churches in our parts. All these I collected and put away, and I replaced them by the Gospels of the Four Evangelists."

Here at last are the statements of an eye witness who was perfectly familiar with the book, who had handled many copies of it, and had minutely examined its contents. As Lightfoot says, " The materials before Theodoret were ample ; the man himself was competent to form a judgment ; and the judgment is explicit." We have here no vague or hearsay evidence. We are told the exact point in which Theodoret held the book unorthodox, the sort of persons of two persuasions who used it, their reason for so doing, the number of copies found in one diocese, and the suppression of these to make way for the Canonical Gospels. And the man who gives us all this information, and who was well acquainted with the past history of his Church, accepted it as an undoubted fact that the work had been compiled by Tatian. Indeed, we may well believe that this very point, its heretical authorship, weighed more with the zealous bishop than any internal defect such as the

---

[1] Haer. Fab. i. 20.

omission of the genealogies ; and that he acted very much as a Romish bishop in Ireland would act at the present day in suppressing the Protestant Bible wholesale just because it was Protestant; the only difference being that the Syrian replaced the "heretical" book by the more "Catholic" form of the Gospel, a precaution which would be deemed quite unnecessary by the Roman prelate.

It is not difficult for us to picture the scenes which took place when Theodoret and his archdeacon and other sub-ordinates went round the diocese of Cyrrhus seeking out the old Harmony, and confiscating it, to the chagrin of the simple parish priests and their simpler flocks, who had been accustomed from infancy to hear from its pages the story of redeeming love. We feel sure it must have been endeared to them as an old-fashioned Church book which had come down to them encased in the love and veneration of ages, and the subject of many stories of the olden days of Syrian Christianity.

Of these stories a specimen may be found in a curious old Syriac composition which has comparatively recently been brought to light. It is called the "Doctrine of Addai," [1] and it gives a kind of romantic account of the founding of the Church of Edessa in the time of good King Abgar.

"And they ministered in the church which Addaeus had built at the order and command of King Abgar, and they were furnished with what belonged to the king and to his nobles with some things for the house of God, and others for the supply of the poor. But a large multitude of people assembled day by day, and came to the prayers of the service, and to the reading of the Old Testament and the New of the Diatessaron." [2]

Now the very least that can be said is, that at the time this romance was written, the Diatessaron must have been the form in which the Gospel was commonly read in the Syrian Churches with which the writer was familiar. [3] And

---

There are two editions. The earlier was prepared by Cureton, and published after his death, in *Ancient Syriac Documents* (London, 1864). The later and more complete edition is that of Dr. Phillips. *The Doctrine of Addai* (London, 1876).

[2] The MS. which Dr. Cureton followed here reads *Ditornon*. This word the editor conjectured to be a corruption of *Diatessaron*, p. 158, note. The conjecture was proved correct by Dr. Phillips' MS., which reads *Diatessaron*. See Lightfoot, p. 1,137, note.

[3] It does not follow because a document is apocryphal that its evidence on a matter of fact is worthless. See Dr. Salmon. *Expositor*, 1887, vol. vi., p. 9.

as the composition may perhaps date back as early as the
third century, this would prove that for nearly two hundred
years the Diatessaron was a well-known book among
the Syrians, and that many ages before the visitation when
the orthodox bishop went round from one parish to another
to suppress it, the simple country folk (like Englishmen at
the time of the Reformation), had been accustomed to gather
round, and drink in attentively the words of eternal life,
which were read from its pages, as it lay upon the desk of
their rural sanctuary.

Nor was the use of the Diatessaron confined to the un-
educated classes.   Two great figures shine out brightly in
the Syrian Church History of the 4th century.   These are
Aphraates, "the Persian sage," and Ephraem, "the Harp
of the Holy Spirit."   The one was a great teacher at Mossul
(Nineveh), about A.D. 340; the other lived and laboured
at Edessa, about twenty years later.

Now we have more or less convincing evidence that each
of these men used the Diatessaron.

The evidence is less certain in the case of Aphraates, but
still it has been found sufficient to satisfy many modern
critics of acknowledged acumen.

The Homilies of Aphraates were published in the original
Syriac by Professor Wright, A.D. 1869, but unfortunately no
English version has as yet appeared.   A valuable introduction however speaks of Aphraates as "sometimes mistaking
the book in which the passage occurs, and at other times
mixing up the words of two or more passages of Scripture,"
and the editor adds, "In a few cases I have not been able
to discover the text at which he aims."

Now Zahn, who has made a special study of Aphraates,
is convinced that the one key to the difficulty of his Gospel
citations is that he used the Diatessaron.   He notices that
Aphraates gives citations from the Gospels in great numbers,
but gives them from one book only, and calls this "the
Gospel of Christ."   Indeed in one passage, speaking of
Christ, he calls him the Word of the Lord, " as is written in
the beginning of the Gospel of Our Lifegiver—In the beginning was the Word."

Now it might be imagined that by "the Gospel of Our Lifegiver," which began with this sentence, Aphraates meant
St. John's Gospel : but this is impossible when we consider
how frequently he cites the others.   Or it might be supposed
that in the Book of the Gospels which he used, St. John held

the first place ; but no such position was ever assigned to St. John's Gospel in any Syriac Evangelium.[1]

The simple explanation is to be found in the words of Bar-Salibi, a Syrian Bishop, who lived at the end of the twelfth century, who distinctly states[2] that the Diatessaron of Tatian began with the opening verse of St. John. But more of this by-and-by.

Much more important is the case of Ephraem. He was the brightest star of the Syrian Church, and the most voluminous writer which it ever produced.[3] Now the same Bar-Salibi, in the same place to which I have referred, distinctly states that Ephraem wrote a commentary on the Diatessaron of Tatian.

"Tatian, the disciple of Justin, the philosopher and martyr, selected and patched together from the Four Gospels and constructed a Gospel which he called *Diatessaron*, that is *Miscellanies*. On this work Mar Ephraem wrote an exposition, and its commencement was—*In the beginning was the word*" (Lightfoot's translation).

It is impossible to over-estimate the value of this evidence ; for the critical discernment of Bar-Salibi is shown by the fact that in the immediate context he distinguishes between this Diatessaron of Tatian, and two others by Ammonius and Elias of Salamia respectively.[4] While his fitness to pronounce on the history of Gospel Commentaries is proved by the fact that he himself was a commentator of no mean rank on the Gospel narrative. So that, as Hug many years ago observed,[5] he was in every way a credible witness. Indeed it was only persons, like the author of "*Supernatural Religion*," who disliked the "*tendency*" of the admission that a compilation of the Four Gospels was made by a second-century writer, a friend of Justin, a man born only twenty years after the death of St. John, who were bold enough to reject the statement of Bar-Salibi as unworthy of credit. But even this sweeping criticism had its blessings for the Church, for it called forth

---

[1] The order of the Gospels in the Curetonian is Mat., Mar., Joh., Luke, while the Peshitto order is the same as our own.

[2] In the preface to his Commentary on St. Mark. A contemporary MS. of the Commentary of Dionysius Bar-Salibi is contained in the Library of Trinity College, Dublin.

[3] Sozomen, Ec. Hist., iii. 16, says that his works contained over 3,000,000 lines

[4] See context in Lightfoot.

[5] Introduction to the N. T., Wait's Trans. Vol. i., p. 47.

that able article of Lightfoot, from which I have so frequently quoted, and which is the best statement of the case for the traditional view of the Diatessaron, which any advocate could well have made at the time of its publication.

III.—THE RECOVERY OF THE DIATESSARON.

" WHAT a pity that Ephraem's Commentary on the Diatessaron is not now forthcoming ! " :—

Such must have been the reflection of many a reader of Dr. Lightfoot's article in May, 1877.

Yet exactly twelve months before, in May, 1876, Dr. Moesinger, Professor of Theology in the University of Salzburg, had affixed his name to the preface of a Latin translation of this very commentary of S. Ephraem, on consigning it to the press,[1] and thus the commentary had been published in Venice the same year, and was doubtless lying on the bookseller's table in that city, at the very time when Western scholars were deploring its loss, and speculating[2] as to what had become of it !

It will be desirable to give a few words of explanation as to the history of this Latin publication.

" At the opening of the 18th century, an Armenian priest named Mechitar, passing into Italy from the Morea, established himself in the small island of San Lazzaro, in the lagoon of Venice, where he founded a community for the education of the Armenian people, through the medium of their own language. Here Armenian youths were trained by Mechitar, and sent out as teachers to their compatriots scattered through the East ; a printing establishment was set up, where Armenian versions of European works were printed for dissemination through Armenia ; and San Lazzaro soon became, what it has ever since remained, the focus of Armenian culture."[3]

---

[1] Evangelii concordantis expositio facta a sancto Ephraemo doctore Syro.   Venetiis, 1876.

[2] " At the time when so great activity prevailed in gathering MSS. for the Vatican, an Egyptian vessel laden with books for Pope Clement XI. unfortunately sank in the Nile, and many of Ephraem's writings were lost, and others rendered illegible."   Dean Payne Smith, in Smith's Dict. of X°. Biog. Art. *Ephraem.*

[3] Extract from a brochure issued from the Mechitarist Monastery Press, in 1877 ; translated for me by Mr. N. Colgan.

The MS. library in connexion with this monastery appears to have been enriched with "some of the most precious relics of early Armenian literature. Amongst others are an Armenian Ritual of the 8th century, the Armenian Bible of Melké, queen of Armenia, written in the year 902," and two 12th century MSS.[1] of an Armenian translation, made apparently in the 5th century from the Syriac, of Ephraem's Commentary on a Gospel Harmony!

How long the Armenian monks have been consciously possessed of this last inestimable treasure we know not, but in 1836 there issued from the Monastery press an Armenian edition of St. Ephraem's works in 4 vols. octavo, the second of which contains the Commentary on the Harmony.[2] Moreover a Latin translation of this last was made so long ago as 1841 by Father Aucher, but it remained unpublished until Moesinger, the Salzburg professor, revised it by the aid of the MSS., and edited it with a preface, as I have said, in 1876.

Yet strange as it is that this Armenian edition of Ephraem's Commentary remained so long unknown to Western scholars, even in such a frequented resort as Venice, it is stranger still that Moesinger's Latin version of it, published in 1876, took five years to penetrate to these islands! Nor did it even cross the Alps, and become known in Germany, the native land of its editor, till about the same time, when having taken a voyage across the Atlantic, and having made the acquaintance of Dr. Ezra Abbot, it was by him introduced to the notice of Western Europe![4]   Well

---

[1] See an account of them in Moesinger's Preface pp. x-xi. By a singular coincidence they were both written A.D. 1195; *i.e.*, in the lifetime of Bar-Salibi.

[2] The learned writer of the art. *Ephraem*, quoted above, after referring to the lost Diatessaron, goes on to mention that the Commentary on the Pauline epp. "may be found in the third vol. of a collection of Armenian translations of Ephraem's works, published in four vols. octavo by the Mechitarists at Venice in 1836." What a pity he did not take up the second volume instead.

[3] Except in a passing notice in Schürer's *Theologische Literaturzeitung*, Dec. 7th, 1878. See Wace, *below*.

[4] In his "Authorship of the Fourth Gospel," 1880. Dr. Harnack reviewed Moesinger's work in the *Zeitschrift für Kirchengeschichte*, Feb. 1881. In the following April it was noticed by Prof. Wace in the *Quarterly Review;* by Prof. G. T. Stokes, in the *Irish Ecclesiastical Gazette;* and by Prof. Westcott, in the 5th ed. of his *History of the Canon of the N.T.* And in the following July Prof. Wace began his series of most valuable articles in the *Expositor.*

has Dr. Wace remarked that our critical materials are beginning to overpower us.

We now come to examine this publication on its own merits.

And first, we have the opinion of experts,[1] that the Armenian was written about the 5th century,[2] and was *a translation from the Syriac.* It seems indeed (fortunately for textual critics), to be a most servile translation, and to retain in a remarkable degree the Syriac idioms and constructions. This fact is well worthy of attention.

Again, there is no doubt that *the authorship is correctly ascribed to S. Ephraem.* His extant works are, in spite of losses, still very voluminous, and internal evidence vindicates the right of this Commentary to a place among them.

It is written in his usual style, which inclines more to the school of Antioch than to that of Alexandria,[3] but yet has been well described[4] as "pious rather than learned." It deals with Scripture in a precisely similar manner to Ephraem's other works, selecting leading texts rather than extensive passages for exposition, and occasionally letting the comments on these run on to very disproportionate length.[5] Sometimes prayers, sometimes poetical words and ideas are introduced ; both of which would agree with Ephraem's turn of mind. Further there are disputations against the Marcionites, whose strenuous opponent Ephraem was, and eulogies of the monastic life, of which he was a devoted admirer.[6] A reference has been noted also to the unhappy schism in the Church of

---

[1] Aucher and Moesinger.

[2] "An age of great intellectual activity in Armenia and Georgia." Prof. Stokes, *l.c.*

[3] Lamy. *S. Ephraem Syri Hymni et Sermones.* Mechlin, 1882. Pref. p. 10, says :—

"Ephraem, like John Chrysostom and Theodoret, follows the method of the school of Antioch, and devotes himself to bringing out the literal sense, which he explains in very short *scholia :* but he always passes over in silence the allegorical explanations which Philo and Origen, masters of the Alexandrian school, always follow, although he does not altogether reject the spiritual meaning, but on the contrary explains many things in a mystic sense, but only in cases where some good reason persuades him such a sense is inherent in the letter."

[4] By Bellarmine.

[5] For instance in the case of John's birth, nine pages, and the woman with the issue, fourteen pages.

[6] I may perhaps quote in the words of Dean Payne Smith, a story told of Ephraem on his arrival at Edessa.

"As he entered the city, a number of women were engaged in washing linen on the banks of the river Daisan, and as one of them

Edessa in Ephraem's time, when the Bishop, Barses, was expelled by the Emperor Valens.[1] And, finally, many coincidences in opinions and ways of expressing them, and in the form of certain words, have been pointed out by Moesinger[2] and Lamy[3] between this Commentary and Ephraem's other works.

Our third point, that *the basis of this Commentary of S. Ephraem is a Gospel Harmony*, is evident to anyone who looks for one moment at the index of passages in the order in which Ephraem comments on them.

It remains then to prove that *this Gospel Harmony is the Diatessaron of Tatian.*

Well, first, Dionysius Bar-Salibi says, that this is so, and considering the means which he had of forming an opinion, the definiteness of the opinion, its inherent probability, and the fact that no evidence can be produced on the other side, we may safely accept it as satisfactory.

Besides everything else which we independently know of the Diatessaron fits in with Bar-Salibi's judgment.

Tatian's Diatessaron was compiled from the four Gospels, nothing being said of other matter (Eusebius); and Ephraem's Harmony is compiled from the four Gospels alone. The Diatessaron of Tatian omitted the genealogies (Theodoret), so does Ephraem's Harmony. The Diatessaron was current in the neighbourhood of Edessa, about the 4th century, and was read there as Scripture (Doctrine of Addai), and Ephraem, the great teacher of Edessa, in the 4th century, employs his Harmony as well known in the Church, and actually calls it "Scripture."

It may be taken as proved therefore that Ephraem in this work comments on Tatian's Diatessaron, and that in the work as published in 1876, we have translations[4] of con-

---

looked at him more intently than seemed becoming, he rebuked her, saying, 'Be modest, O woman, and fix thy look upon the ground.' ' It is quite right,' she answered 'for men to look upon the ground, for out of it they were taken : but for the same reason I may surely look at thee, for woman was taken out of man.' 'If the women here,' he said, as he passed on 'are so wise, what must the men be ?"

[1] p. 284.

[2] Preface, p. viii.   Notes, pp. 18 note 4., 24 note 1., 36 note 1., 57 note 4., 194 note 1., 220 note 2.

[3] Proleg. 75 note 2., 86 note 2., 87.   Also pp. 12 note., 129 note 1., 175 note, 359 note, 423 note 1., 687 note 1., volume ii. p. 539 note.

[4] Not only does the Armenian seem to be a literal rendering of its Syriac exemplar, but Moesinger professes to have been most careful to preserve a like exactness in translating the Armenian into Latin (Pref. xi., *ad. fin.*)

siderable fragments[1] of the Diatessaron, as it existed in the 4th century. The great critical value of these fragments will occupy our attention hereafter,[2] but for the present we must go on to consider how they lead still further to the recovery of the whole work of Tatian.

It will be remembered that Victor, Bishop of Capua, in the year 543, found a Latin Harmony or Compilation of the four Gospels without any name or title : and being a man of enquiring mind he at once set about the task of discovering its unknown author. I have already mentioned the way in which from the passage of Eusebius he was led to ascribe his discovery to Tatian. This conclusion was generally traversed by Church writers, and Victor was supposed to have made a mistake.[3] He is now however proved to have been a better judge than his critics, for, as Dr. Wace was the first to point out, a comparison of this Latin Harmony with the Ephraem fragments demonstrates their substantial identity, as they preserve to a wonderful degree the same order, and generally proceed *pari passu.*

At the same time it must be remembered that this applies only to the contents and their order, not to the text adopted. The Latin Harmony, as it now exists in the Codex Fuldensis, represents not the Harmony as it was found by Victor, but the Harmony as it was modified and edited under his direction.[4] The Index, which somehow escaped revision, does not in all cases agree with the body of the Codex,[5] from which we gather that the latter may have been to some extent changed in order, and interpolated as in the case of the genealogies : while the text which Victor found

---

[1] In the Armenian MSS. which Moesinger used it appears that the passages forming the basis of the commentary of Ephraem are written in vermilion. (Moesinger, p. 90, note 4, p. 108, note 4.) In the Latin edition these passages are printed in spaced type ; and there can be no doubt that, with slight exceptions perhaps, they are a faithful representation of the fragments of Tatian's work which Ephraem embodied in his commentary.

[2] Appendix E. The bearing of these fragments on textual criticism was fully recognized by Moesinger (Pref. ix, x), who noticed their similarity to the text of the Curetonian Syriac, and expressed his intention of discussing this in a separate treatise. But death prevented him. This work has since been very ably accomplished by Bäthgen, *Der Griechische Text des Cureton'schen Syrers* (Leipzig, 1885). See also Zahn, pp. 220 foll.

[3] Even so late as A.D. 1868 when Ranke published the Cod. Fuldensis.

[4] See Mr. Daniell's art. *Victor*, in Smith D.C.B. vol. 4., p. 1125.

[5] For instance § 70 in the Cod. answers to § 68 in the Index. And §§ 105, 106 in the Index have by a mistake the same titles as §§ 95, 96.

has been changed piece by piece into the Vulgate of St. Jerome.[1]

Again the rude and ungrammatical nature of the Latin preserved in the Index,[2] and which presumably extended before revision to the whole Harmony, would lead us to suppose that it was an ignorant translation from some other language, probably Syriac.[3] And this is highly probable for other reasons. For at the end of the 5th century (*i.e.* shortly before the time of Victor) there existed causes for closer intercourse between the Syrian and Latin Churches. Pilgrimages from West to East became fashionable; the Nestorian and Eutychian controversies had produced more friction between East and West, the Syrian schools of theology began to be taken as a model for similar institutions at Rome and elsewhere; and there is evidence of increasing familiarity with the Syriac language on the part of Western writers.[4] There is nothing strange therefore in the existence of a Latin version of the Syriac Diatessaron just at this particular time. The strange thing is that this should have been current in the Western Church for over 1300 years, sometimes even with the name of Tatian on its title page,[5] and yet that no one would believe that it was the Heretic's workmanship, until the conviction was driven home by Moesinger's publication. So that we have now found the Diatessarron only to find that we always possessed it! How full of curious and unexpected turns is the history of this remarkable book!

---

[1] Of which according to Tischendorf it is the next best MS. after the Cod. Amiatinus.

[2] For instance, § 9. *Ubi infugatus Jhesus et parentes ejus in aegypto.*
§ 31. *de oculum pro oculo.*
§ 43. *de sapiente et insipiente aedificatoribus.*
§ 53. *Ubi curavit trans fretum daemoniacum qui in monumentis manebant.*
§ 57. *Ubi scribae signum petunt ab eo et eis multa dicit.*
§ 66. *Ubi apostoli revertuntur ad Jhesum de praedicationem.*
§ 69. *Ubi Jhesus in montem orat.*
§ 73. *De fermento quod abscondit mulier et alia multa discipulis.*
§ 89. *Ubi Jhesus de vii. panes et paucos pisces iv. hominum saturavit.*
§ 91. *Ubi Jhesus dicit et quidam astantibus non gustare mortem.*
§ 150. *Ut lumbi semper praecincti sint et lucernae ardentes.*

[3] Dr. Gwynn, however, points out that the occurence in these *Capita* (cxx.) of the *pericope de adulteria* is a serious argument against their supposed Syriac origin.

[4] See Zahn p. 312, note 2. Wace, *Expositor*, 1882. vol. ii. p. 294. Daniell *l. c.*

[5] In most of the editions of the Latin Harmony, and in the old Saxon translation of this.

Hitherto we have seen that in the very same century (the 5th), in which Theodoret did all in his power to suppress the Diatessaron in the land of its birth, it was beginning to spread abroad, like all persecuted things, and to embrace within the circle of its influence such widely opposite regions as Armenia and Italy ; in the one case through a translation of the Commentary which Ephraem had written on it ; in the other through an anonymous, and probably barbarous Latin version, both of which have just been shown to be indirectly available for literary purposes.

A period of over four hundred years must now be over leaped, during which we hear nothing of the Diatessaron, and we must come to that era when the whole of Syria had submitted to the Saracen yoke, and when the Syrians, forgetting their mother tongue, like the Jews at Babylon, and again at Alexandria, long ages before,[1] found it necessary to have their Scriptures and other sacred books translated into Arabic, the language of their conquerors. We have clear proof that the Diatessaron shared this fortune, and indeed it is from the Arabic alone that it can now be recovered in its integrity.

It was stated at the beginning of this Introduction that an Arabic book bearing the title of "Tatian's Harmony" had this year been given to the literary world.[2] It is now necessary to give a somewhat more detailed account of this. It is drawn from two manuscripts. Of these, the first has long been known to exist in the Vatican Library,[3] but surprisingly little definite information about it was forthcoming even so recently as A.D. 1881, when Zahn's great monograph issued from the press. Zahn in fact knew nothing of this MS. except what he had gleaned from the writings of the three scholars, S. E. Assemani, Rosenmüller and Akerblad.[4] And the unsatisfactory nature of their information is apparent on the face of it. To begin with, the notices are extremely meagre. Assemani's description occupies only a few lines,[5] while the Latin translations of Rosenmüller and Akerblad (to judge from Zahn's account of them), are merely specimens from the first leaf or so of the Codex. But besides being meagre, these authorities were found to contradict one another ; for while Assemani averred that almost half of the

---

[1] The cause of the Targums and the Septuagint respectively. page vii.
[3] Cod. Vat. Arab. xiv.
[4] Zahn, pp. 294-298.
[5] In Mai's Script. vet. n. col., iv. 2. 14.

Codex was destroyed with moths and damp, Akerblad said
that it was perfect, except for the damage of a few leaves at
the beginning. Again, as to the words with which the Codex
began, Rosenmüller thought that the first verse of St. Mark
stood first, while the other two treated this as a mere pre-
fatory gloss.

Still, for all these drawbacks, important facts could be
learned from these authorities as to the nature and value of
the Codex. In the first place it was shown to contain a note
in which it professed to be a translation of Tatian's Diàtes-
saron.[1] Next it bore evident signs of having been translated
from the Syriac.[2] And finally it plainly contained traces of
interpolation and textual revision.[3]

The attention which Zahn's work was the means of
directing to this Arabic Diatessaron caused Ciasca, one of
the Scribes of the Vatican library, in a dissertation which he
wrote in 1883, to give a more worthy description of the
MS., and, better still, a promise that if ever he had leisure
he would publish it in full.[4] Other engagements however
delayed the fulfilment of this promise, and in 1885 he handed
over a copy which he had made from the MS. to de Lagarde,
who had conceived a wish to be its editor. But he too was
prevented through want of time and type, and the responsibility again devolved on Ciasca. This delay, however annoy-
ing, turned out to be providential. For next year Antonius
Morcos, Vicar Apostolic of the Catholic Copts, happened to
be staying at Rome, and on being shown the MS. among
other Vatican treasures by Ciasca, declared that he had seen
a similar one, and that it was in the possession of a member
of his communion in Egypt. This second MS.[5] was without
delay (August, 1886) forwarded to Rome. and Ciasca goes
on to describe it as a most elegant specimen of caligraphy,
written in the Oriental style, consisting of 355 leaves, and
beautifully embellished with gold and colours. Indeed it

[1] Assemani thus renders this note which is at the end of the 123rd
leaf :—Explicit auxilio Dei sacrosanctum evangelium, quod ex quatuor
evangeliis collegit Tatianus, quodque Diatessaron vulgo dicitur. Et
laus Deo.

[2] Akerblad says :—"As far as the Arabic version is concerned I have
no doubt that it was made from some Syriac exemplar ; for everything
in this version savours of the Syriac, and the titles of chapters or sections
show a Syrian author."

For instance, the genealogies.

[4] In Pitra's *Analecta Sacra.* See Introduction to the Arabic
Diatessaron. Rome 1888, p. v.

[5] Called by Ciasca "Codex Borgianus."

was the exquisite character of its writing and ornamentation which induced the Vatican scribes to select this MS. for publication, as the most appropriate present which they could offer to Pope Leo XIII. on the occasion of his Jubilee.

The first eighty-five leaves consist of a kind of preface to the Gospels which is written in a very learned but apparently prolix style, and contains citations from Zoroaster, Aristotle, Ammonius, Eusebius and others. Passing on to the text, it is found to contain material for supplying the numerous *lacunae* of the Vatican Codex ; again, it is free from the interpolations noticed in the latter ;[1] and it contains notes at the beginning and end in which the reader is informed that this is an Arabic translation of Tatian's Diatessaron, that it was made from the Syriac, and that the translator was " the most learned Presbyter Abû-l-Pharag Abdullah Ben-at-Tîb ;" the note at the end supplying also the name of the scribe of the Syriac exemplar as Isa ben Alì Almotattabbeb, the disciple of Honain ben Ishac.

Assemani,[2] who derives his information chiefly from Barhebraeus, tells us that this Ben-at-Tîb was by race an Assyrian, and by profession a monk and presbyter of the Nestorians, that he flourished at the beginning of the eleventh century and died A.D. 1043. This information, if reliable, would give us an approximate date for the translation into Arabic ; while the date of Honain's death, A.D. 873,[3] enables us to form some idea of the period at which his disciple, Isa ben Ali, must have copied the Syriac MS. which came into Ben-at-Tib's hands.

Thus we see that up to the eleventh century, in which Ben-at-Tib was alive, there was preserved in the native land of Tatian and Ephraem a Syriac work bearing the name of the Diatessaron. Was it then the same Diatessaron upon which Ephraem wrote his commentary? A comparison of the works edited by Moesinger and Ciasca respectively, proves conclusively that so far as contents and arrangement are concerned, the two represent one and the same harmony. Not only is there the same general agreement which was noticed between the Ephraem fragments and the Latin harmony found by Victor, but down to the very smallest detail, except in four instances,[4] the order in which passages

---

[1] It gives the genealogies at the end as a sort of appendix under the title " The book of the generation of Jesus."

[2] Bibl. Or. T. iii., par. 1, p. 544.

[3] Ciasca, p. 13, note,

[4] §§ 8. 15. 50. 106. in the present edition.

of the Gospels are cited by Ephraem, is the order in which they occur in the Arabic Harmony. But while the contents and arrangement of the ninth century Diatessaron are so nearly identical with those of the fourth century, thus showing a continuous existence of Tatian's work, the texts are completely different. The strong Curetonian element present in the Ephraem fragments[1] seems to have been almost entirely eliminated from the type which Isa-ben-Ali copied, and Ben-at-Tib translated, so that we gain the interesting information that between the fourth and ninth centuries the Syriac Diatessaron must have undergone a revision somewhat analogous to that by which we know that the bald and rugged renderings of the Victorian Harmony were toned down into the Hieronymian Latin of the Codex Fuldensis. While therefore the Arabic probably represents Tatian's patchwork in its true proportions, and gives us a correct view of his arrangement of the Evangelical narratives, it cannot be said to preserve the text which he used, or the curious and original turns which he gave to the words of the sacred writers. For these we must go back to the Ephraem fragments and the Gospel citations of Aphraates.[2]

These considerations will sufficiently explain the principle adopted in the present edition. The Arabic version, as represented by Ciasca's Latin (**A**c), has been accepted as a trustworthy witness of the scope, material and arrangement of Tatian's work ;[3] while the fragments contained in Ephraem's Commentary, as represented by Moesinger's Latin rendering of the Armenian (**E**m), have been collected, translated into English, and arranged, as furnishing, even through a threefold version,[4] specimens of the type of text which Tatian used.

The sections into which the Diatessaron has been divided have generally been suggested by manifest changes of subject, or breaks in the continuity of a narrative.[5] Some of these

---

1 See p. xxiv., Note 2.

2 It is interesting to note that the fragments of Tatian's work contained in the Homilies of Aphraates are the only ones which do not come to us through the medium of a translation. They are the *ipsissima verba* of Tatian. See Harnack, *Texte und Untersuchungen, &c.* Leipzig, 1883. *Die Acta Archelai und das Diatessaron Tatian's*, p. 139.

3 I have indicated the passages of the Gospels according to the ordinary notation, following the guidance of Ciasca, only abbreviating the names of the Evangelists thus :—M. Mar. L. J.

4 Armenian, Latin and English.

5 The chapters into which the Diatessaron is divided in the Arabic, and in Ephraem, are manifestly too long for the purposes of this edition.

are to be gathered from **A**ₑ others from **E**ₘ, others again from the Codex Fuldensis. The titles are in some cases suggested by the Victorian *Capita.*

It remains that something should be said as to the principle which Tatian followed,. and the object which he had in view in compiling his Diatessaron.

On the first point the Arabic version is a very clear addition to our knowledge. On examining the Diatessaron as translated into Latin from this Arabic, we find in by far the greater portion of it, from the Sermon on the Mount to the Last Supper (§§ 30-134), that Tatian, like his brother harmonist Ammonius, took St. Matthew as the basis of his work.[1] Thus in the sections I have mentioned the order of chapters of St. Matthew is as follows :—

5. 6. 7. 8. 9. 10. 11. 12. 16. 11. 12. 13. 14. 15. 16. 17. 18. 19. 18. 19. 20. 22. 20. 21. 22. 26. 21. 23. 24. 25. 26.

It is thus clear that if we take the passages of St. Matthew which are incorporated in the Diatessaron, in the exact order in which we there find them, they will very fairly represent the order of the Evangelist himself. St. Mark, as might be expected, runs tolerably parallel with St. Matthew in the Diatessaron, and is in a few cases the source out of which incidents have been incorporated. St. Luke on the other hand is employed by Tatian, as also in a lesser degree is St. John, in complete defiance of chronological order. In the above-named sections the order of St. Luke's chapters is as follows :—

6. 12. 7. 9. 8. 9. 12. 10. 7. 16. 11. 7. 10. 14. 11. 8. 13. 4. 9. 11. 5. 9. 13. 9. 19. 9. 14. 15. 16. 17. 12. 13. 12. 18. 16. 14. 17. 18. 13. 19. 18. 19. 21. 18. 9. 17. 18. 20. 10. 19. 9. 19. 17. 21. 11. 21. 19. 21. 12. 22.

Indeed it is now quite plain that the extraordinary anachronisms and other peculiarities in order, which have been pointed out in the Diatessaron, are mainly due to the principle on which Tatian inserted in the text of S. Matthew passages from SS. Luke and John.[2] In fact he seems to have

---

[1] See p. xv., note 1. It is possible that Ammonius derived the name of his work (Diatessaron) and even the idea of it from having heard somehow of Tatian's Harmony. See Zahn, p. 31, foll.

[2] Thus from S. Luke he incorporates the Episode about Martha and Mary (§ 40), the mission of the 70 (§ 47), and the Parables of the Tower and the King (§ 48) much too early; while the Rejection at Nazareth (§ 58) is much too late. Notice also how (§ 75) Herod's threat is inserted between the Transfiguration and the cure of the demoniac boy : and how the Episode about the slain Galileans (§ 87) is put after the parable of the Prodigal Son. Again looking at the insertions from S. John, the discourse with the woman of Samaria (§ 66), and the cure of

treated these last named Gospels as mere material for filling up his patchwork, a process which he regulated according to ethical, not chronological considerations. Sometimes he incorporated passages which seemed to teach the same spiritual truth,[1] at other times he was influenced by a love of contrast.[2] The truth probably is that here we have the work of a man whose sole object was the spiritual edification of his readers, and we are insensibly reminded of that exiled teacher, who, when the imperial city became too hot to hold him,[3] went forth a friendless outcast to find a congenial sphere of work on the banks of the remote Euphrates, among his heathen fellow-countrymen. There, like Missionaries of the present day, he would soon find it expedient to prepare a vernacular Gospel to leave behind him ; and we can imagine him choosing for that purpose not one of the four Canonical Gospels, as a believer in verbal inspiration would have done, but, like a bold and original man, a patchwork of his own piecing, which would both comprise every important event in the Saviour's history, and at the same time present that history in a form free from seeming contradictions.

---

the impotent man at Bethesda (§ 68) are put after the discourse on the Bread of Life (§ 62). The second chapter of S. John is found so late as § 102, because the two cleansings of the temple are confounded ; and the visit of Nicodemus is recorded (§ 106), after the cursing of the fig tree, evidently showing that Tatian utterly disregarded the chronological data of S. John, and apparently compressed Our Lord's ministry into one year. Compare below, p. 64.

[1] See §§ 47 and 48 : 50 and 51 : 90. 91. 92. 93. and 94 : 98 and 99 : 113 and 114: 131 and 132.

[2] Compare Herod's threat and the visit of Nicodemus, which seem to contrast with their immediate context.

[3] p. vii.

TATIAN'S GOSPEL DIATESSARON.

THE CONTENTS INDICATED ACCORDING TO THE ARABIC,
AND THE FRAGMENTS CONTAINED IN THE
COMMENTARY OF EPHRAEM SYRUS
TRANSLATED AND ARRANGED.

A LIST OF ABBREVIATIONS.

A.—The Arabic Diatessaron edited and translated into Latin by Ciasca. Rome, 1888.

E.—The Commentary of Ephraem Syrus translated into Latin from the Armenian by Moesinger. Venice, 1876.

M.—S. Matthew: Mar.—S. Mark: L.—S. Luke: J.—S. John.

Sc.—The Curetonian Syriac according to Cureton's English Translation. London, 1858.

Pesh.—The Peshitto according to Etheridge's English Translation. London, 1846.

T.—Tatian.

E.—Ephraem.

WH—Westcott and Hort's Ed. of the Greek Testament. Cambridge, 1882.

Zahn.—Zahn's Tatian's Diatessaron. Erlangen, 1881.

Greek and Latin Biblical MSS. according to the usual notation.

a, b, or c after a Gospel reference indicates the beginning, middle, or end of a verse.

Words included in brackets are printed in ordinary, not in spaced type in **E.**; and it is doubtful whether the original Diatessaron contained them or not.

§ 1. IN THE BEGINNING WAS THE WORD.

A.–J. i. 1–5.

E. 3–6.

From the beginning [1] was the Word : this Word was with
God, and God was the Word. This was from the beginning
with God. All things through him were made, and without
him was made nothing. Whatsoever was made through
him was life,[2] and the life was the light of men. And this
light was shining [3] in the darkness, and the darkness over-
came it not.

✠

§ 2. THE BIRTH OF THE FORERUNNER. THE ANNUNCIA-
TION.

A.–L. i. 5–80.

E. 6–20.

There was in the days of Herod, King of Judaea, a
certain priest, and his name Zacharias, and his wife Elizabeth.
They were blameless in all their habitation. Thy prayer
has been heard before God : and thou shalt have joy and
exultation. Wine and strong drink he shall not drink. To
turn the hearts of the fathers to the sons : he will prepare
for the Lord a perfect people. How can this be so?
Elizabeth hid herself . . .

In the sixth month . . . of the house of David.

The Lord God shall give him the throne of David his
father. And Elizabeth thy sister hath conceived in her old
age. (This month is the sixth to her.)

Behold I am the handmaid of the Lord, let it be to me
according to thy word.

Blessed art thou among women and blessed is the fruit of
thy womb. Whence to me this, that the mother of my
Lord has come to me? May she be blessed (*v.l.* She shall
be blessed) who believeth, because there shall be a fulfilling
of all [4] words which were spoken to her by the Lord.

My soul doth magnify the Lord . . . from this all genera-
tions shall call me blessed.

And thou, child, shalt be called the prophet of the

---

[1] *v.l.* In the beginning.
[2] Sc. without him even not one thing was. But that which was in
him is life.
[3] Sc. was shining.
[4] "all." source unknown.

A

highest, thou shalt go before the Lord to prepare his ways ; to give perfect knowledge of salvation. By which will appear to us the sun rising from on high, to illuminate our darkness. Who were sitting in darkness and in the shadow of death; to direct our feet into the ways of peace.

⚜

§ 3. Joseph and the Angel.

A.—M. i. 18-25.

E_m 20-26.

The birth of Jesus Christ was thus: When his mother Mary had been betrothed to Joseph, and before she had been given to her husband,[1] she was found with child of the Holy Spirit. Joseph who was a just man[2] was unwilling to traduce Mary. Wherefore there appeared to him an angel, and said, Fear not to receive Mary. He was dwelling in holiness[3] with her until she brought forth her first born. He took her.[4]

✠

§ 4. The Scenes at Bethlehem. The Presentation in the Temple.

A_c—L. ii. 1-39.

E_m 26-29.

Each one was being registered in his own town.

To-day has been born to you a Saviour (which is the Christ of the Lord[5]).

Glory in the highest, and peace in earth (from free will : hope to good sons of men[6]).

Now lettest thou thy servant depart in peace ; behold mine eyes have seen thy mercy, which thou hast prepared before all peoples. Behold this (*child*) stands for fall and for rising again, and for a sign of contradiction ; and thine own soul a sword shall go through.

---

[1] Probably an euphemism of T. (Zahn.)
[2] Sc. but Joseph because he was a righteous man.
[3] Sc. purely dwelt with her.
[4] Source unknown.
[5] " of the Lord " found also in Jerusalem Syriac.
[6] These words in brackets are not in large type in E_m ; it is impossible to tell whether T. originally read them or not.

§ 5. The Magi and the Flight into Egypt.

A_c—M. ii. 1-23.

E_m 29-36.

(The star appeared.)   And I will come, I will adore him.
And they opened their treasures, and presented to him gifts,
gold and myrrh and frankincense.[1]   And they received in
a vision the command that they should not return to him.

Then was fulfilled the word which was spoken through the
prophet, who said, Out of Egypt have I called (*v.l.* will I
call) my son.

And when Herod saw that he was mocked by the Magi,
he was very angry, and sent and destroyed all the male
children.   The word was being fulfilled[2] which was spoken
through Jeremiah, A voice was heard in Rama, Rachel was
lamenting her sons, because they were not.

A Nazarene he shall be called.

✠

§ 6. Jesus at the Age of Twelve.

A_c—L. ii. 40-52.

E_m 40.

I and thy father, sorrowing and grieving were going and
seeking thee.[3]

In the house of my Father I must be.

✠

§ 7. John's Preaching of Repentance.

A_c—L. iii. 1-3 : M. iii. 1-3 : L. iii. 4-6.

E_m *No ref.*

✠

§ 8. John's Testimony to Christ.

A_c—J. i. 7-28.

E_n 36-39.

And the Word became flesh and dwelt in us.   Through
Moses is the law, but its truth through Jesus our Lord (36).
Grace and truth came through Jesus (7).   The Jews sent to

---

[1] Sc. gold and myrrh and frankincense.
[2] Sc. then was fulfilled the word . . .
[3] Sc. with anxiety and much grief were seeking thee.

John, and say to him, Who art thou? He confessed,
saying, I am not the Christ.[1]   They say to him, Art thou
Elias? He says, No.

✠

§ 9.   John's Baptism.   Jesus is Baptized.

Ac—M. iii. 4-10 : L. iii. 10-18 : M. iii. 13 : L. iii. 23 : J. i. 29-31 :
   M. iii. 14, 15 : L. iii. 21[b] : M. iii. 16[b] : L. iii. 22[a] : M. iii. 17 :
   J. i. 32-34.

Eₘ 39-42.

And in a garment of the hairs of a camel was John
clothed.   From these stones God is able to raise up sons of
Abraham.   Behold the axe has come even to the root of
the tree.

Behold this is the Lamb of God, this is he who comes to
take away the sins of the world.[2]

And Jesus himself was of years as it were thirty.

Permit now that we may fulfil all righteousness.[3]

✠

§ 10.   The Temptation.

Ac—L. iv. 1[a] : Mar. i. 12, 13[b] : M. iv. 2[a] : L. iv. 2[b] : M. iv. 2[b]-7 :
   L. iv. 5-7 : M. iv. 10 : L. iv. 13 : M. iv. 11[b].

Eₘ 42-49.

Immediately the Holy Spirit led him forth into the desert
that he should be tempted by the devil.   And after he fasted
forty days he desired to eat.[4]   If thou art the Son of God,
speak to these stones, that they become bread this moment.
Not by bread alone doth man live, but by every word which
proceedeth out of the mouth of God.   He led him forth,
and stationed him above the corner of the temple . . . cast
thyself downwards to the earth, for it is written that they
shall guard thee, lest at any time thy foot should strike
against a stone.

---

[1] Sc. and he confessed and said that I am not the Messiah.

[2] Sc. lo the lamb of God ! Lo he that beareth the sin of the world.
" who comes," probably T.'s own addition. (Zahn.)

[3] E. in his comment refers to the traditional light, which sprang up
over the waters, at the same time that the voice came from heaven, at
Our Lord's baptism : Zahn thinks that he found this originally in T.
but A. has no trace of it.

[4] Sc. and after forty days that he was fasting he was hungry.

Again he took him, and led him to a certain mountain, very high, and says to him, Mine are all kingdoms . . . to me it has been given . . . I have power over all these things . . . thou wilt fall upon thy face, and wilt adore me prostrate, I will give the kingdoms and glory of them to thee. Go behind me Satan.[1] He departed from him for a certain time. Angels came and were ministering to him.

✠

§ 11. THE FIVE DISCIPLES.
Ac—J. i. 35-51.
Em 49-51.

We have found the Christ. This is the Christ. Can it be that anything good should go forth from Nazareth? Behold a true Israelite Scribe in whom is no guile.

✠

§ 12. THE FIRST MIRACLE.
Ac—L. iv. 14 : J. ii. 1-11,
Em 52-57.

A marriage was celebrated in Cana of the Galileans, and when the Lord came there his mother says to him, They have no wine here. Jesus says to her, What is it to me and to thee, Madam? My time has not yet arrived. Whatsoever my son shall say to you do it. Every man first serves up good wine, afterwards light wine.

✠

§ 13. JESUS PREACHES AT NAZARETH AND OTHER PLACES.
Ac—L. iv. 14b-22a : M. iv. 17a : Mar. i. 15.
Em 57.

The times[2] are fulfilled (Mar. i. 15.)

✠

§ 14. THE CALLING OF DISCIPLES AT THE SEA.
Ac—M. iv. 18-22.
Em *No ref.*

---

[1] Sc. get thee behind me Satan.
[2] Sc. wanting, but D. Itt. which often agree with it have the plural like T.

§ 15.   The Miraculous Draught of Fishes,
A$_c$—L. v. 1-11.

E$_m$ 59.
(Two ships).   We have toiled the whole night.
They made signs to their companions.

✠

§ 16.   John again testifies to Christ.
A$_c$—J. iii. 22–iv. 3.

E$_m$ 58.
His disciples were baptizing (J. iv, 2).

✠

§ 17.   John Imprisoned.
A$_c$—L. iii. 19, 20 : M. iv. 12.

E$_m$ *No ref.*

✠

§ 18 Nobleman's Son at Capernaum.
A$_c$—J. iv. 46–54.

E$_m$ *No ref.*

✠

§ 19.   Jesus goes to Zebulun and Naphtali.
A$_c$—L. iv. 44 : M. iv. 13–16.

E$_m$ *No ref.*

✠

§ 20.   Demoniac in Synagogue.
A$_c$—L. iv. 31^b–37.

E$_m$ *No ref.*

✠

§ 21.   Call of Matthew the Publican.
A$_c$—L. iv. 38^a : M. ix. 9^b.

E$_m$ *See § 24.*

§ 22. CHRIST CURES PETER'S MOTHER-IN-LAW AND MANY OTHERS.

A$_c$—Mar. i. 29: L. iv. 38^b, 39: M. viii. 16: L. iv. 40^b: M. viii. 17:
Mar. i. 33: L. iv. 41.

E$_m$ *No ref.*

✠

§ 23. CHRIST MINISTERS THROUGHOUT THE COUNTRY.

A$_c$—Mar. i. 35-38: L. iv. 42^b, 43: M. ix. 35: Mar. i. 39^b:
L. iv. 14^b, 15.

E$_m$ *No ref.*

✠

§ 24. CALL OF LEVI, THE SON OF ALPHAEUS.

A$_c$—Mar. ii. 14.

E$_m$ 58.

(*No distinct quotation*)[1].

✠

§ 25. THE PARALYTIC LET DOWN THROUGH THE ROOF.

A$_c$—M. iv. 24: Mar ii. 1, 2: L. v. 17^b-21: Mar ii. 8-12^a: L v. 25^b:
M. ix. 8^b: L. v. 26^b: Mar. ii. 12^b.

E$_m$ 59, 60.

The Lord sees their faith . . . says to him, Thy sins are forgiven thee.

✠

§ 26. LEVI'S FEAST. ON FASTING.

A$_c$—L. v. 27-36^b: Mar. ii. 21, 22: L. v. 38^b, 39.

E$_m$ 61.

(The Pharisees and Scribes murmur and say, Ye eat and drink with publicans and sinners. To whom the Lord said, They that are whole have no need of the physician, but they that are sick; and I did not come to call the just but sinners.)

The companions of the bridegroom cannot fast while the bridegroom is with them.

---

[1] The words of E$_m$ 58 are "*Elegit Jacobum publicanum, ut animus adderetur sociis ejus Christum sequendi.*"
This evidently proves that T. read Mar. ii. 14, according to the Western reading "James the son of Alphaeus" for "Levi, the son of Alphaeus." See W. H. *in loc.*

§ 27. PLUCKING EARS OF CORN ON THE SABBATH.

A$_c$—M. xii. 1, 2^a : Mar. ii. 24^b–27 : M. xii. 5–8.

E$_m$ 61, 62.

They began to pluck the ears of corn, and to rub them, and eat.[1]

Behold thy disciples do, on the Sabbath day, that which is not lawful to do.

The Sabbath was made for men.

Their priests in the temple profane the Sabbath and are guiltless.

✠

§ 28. HIS FRIENDS THINK HIM INSANE.

A$_c$—Mar. iii. 21.

E$_m$ *No ref.*

✠

§ 29. WITHERED HAND CURED ON THE SABBATH.   THE PHARISEES CONSPIRE.

A$_c$—L. vi. 6–9 : Mar. iii. 4^b, 5 : M. xii. 11, 12, 14–21.

E$_m$ *No ref.*

✠

§ 30. JESUS PRAYS ON A MOUNTAIN, AND SELECTS THE TWELVE.

A$_c$—L. vi. 12, 13 : Mar. iii. 7^b–12 : L. vi. 18^b, 19 : M. v. 1^a : L. vi. 13^b–17 : Mar. iii. 14, 15.

E$_m$ *No ref.*[2]

---

[1] Sc. began plucking the ears, and rubbing in their hands, and eating.

[2] E$_m$, p. 51, contains the following words in large type :—
    "*Ordo et Solemnitas Apostolorum Domini*" :
on which the note says : " The following words have been taken out of some kind of Ecclesiastical book : 'This inscription is wanting in Cod. B.' "

§ 31. THE SERMON ON THE MOUNT.

A.—L. vi. 20ᵃ : M. v. 2-10 : L. vi. 22ᵃ : M. v. 11ᵇ, 12 : L. vi. 24-27ᵃ :
M. v. 13-16 : Mar. iv. 22, 23 : M. v. 17-25ᵃ : L. xii. 58ᵇ : M. v.
25ᵇ-42 : L. vi. 30ᵇ, 31 : M. v. 43-46ᵃ : L. vi. 32ᵇ-36 : M. v. 47-
vi. 8 : L. xi. 1ᵇ, 2ᵃ : M. vi. 9-18 : L. xii. 32, 33 : M. vi. 19 23 :
L. xi. 35, 35 : M. vi. 24-27 : L. xii. 26 : M. vi. 28ᵇ-31 : I. xii.
29ᵇ : M. vi. 32-vii. 1 : L. vi. 37ᵇ, 38 : Mar. iv. 24ᵇ, 25 : L. vi.
39-42 : M. vii. 6 : L. xi. 5-13 : M. vii. 12-16ᵃ : L. vi. 44 :
M. vii. 17, 18 : L. vi. 45 : M. vii. 19-23 : L. vi. 47, 48ᵃ : M. vii.
25-27.

E., 62-73.

Jesus lifted up his eyes toward them, and began to
say :—
Blessed are the poor in their spirit :[1]
Blessed are the meek :[2]
Blessed is he who hungers and thirsts after righteousness :
Blessed are they who are of clean heart, for they shall see
God :
Blessed are the peacemakers, for they shall be called the
sons of God :
Blessed are they who suffer persecution on account of
righteousness :
Rejoice ye and exult, for great is your reward in heaven.
Woe to you that are rich.
Ye are the light of the world, and ye are the salt of the
earth.
I came not to annul the law or the prophets, but to fulfil.
It is easier for heaven and earth to pass away, than that
one little horn should perish from the law.
Every one who shall have broken one of the commandments. . . . Unless your righteousness be found more
abundant than that of the Scribes and Pharisees, ye shall
not be able to enter into the kingdom of the heavens.
Ye have heard this that has been said, Thou shalt not
kill, for he who kills is liable to the judgment. But I say to
you, he who says to his brother, Absurdly—Low fellow—
or Fool. . . .
If thou art about to offer thy gift on the altar, leave thy
gift and go be reconciled.
Ye have heard that it has been said, Thou shalt not com-
mit adultery : But I say to you, Whosoever looks and lusts

---

[1] Sc. poor in their spirit.
[2] Sc. also puts the beatitude of "the meek" immediately after that
of "the poor in their spirit."

commits adultery.[1]   If thy hand or thy foot causes thee to stumble. . . .

Ye have heard that it has been said, " Eye for eye."   But I say to you, Do not in any wise resist evil : he who strikes thy cheek, offer to him also the other part.[2]

But thou when thou fastest wash thy face and anoint thy head,[3] that thou appear not to men fasting.   Thy Father who seeth in secret shall reward thee openly.

Where your treasures are, there will your hearts be also. If the light which is in thee be darkness. . . .

Judge not lest ye be judged ; forgive and it shall be forgiven you.   Punish not.[4]

Give not holy things to the dogs.

He who has, it shall be given to him ; and he who has not, even that which he thinks he has, shall they take away from him. (L. viii. 18.)

✠

§ 32. The Centurion's Servant.

A.--M. vii. 28–viii. 1, 5ᵃ : L. vii. 2, 3 : M. viii. 5ᵇ, 6 : L. vii. 4, 5 :
    M. viii. 7, 8 : L. vii. 8, 9ᵃ : M. viii. 10ᵇ-13 : L. vii. 10.

E. 74.

He came with the elders of the people (M. and L.) and asked him that he would not refuse to come and heal his servant.   And when he consented to enter, he said to him, Lord trouble not thyself, but only say in a word, and he will be healed.   And when he had heard this, he wondered, and said, Not in anyone in Israel have I found such great faith.[5] . . . they shall go into the outer darkness.

✠

§ 33. The Young Man at Nain.
A.—L. vii. 11-17.

E. 74. *No distinct Quotation.*

---

[1] Sc. that whosoever seeth a woman and lusteth for her, hath committed, &c.

[2] Sc. whoso smiteth thee on thy cheek [turn] to him the other.

[3] Sc. wash thy face and anoint thy head.

[4] Source unknown.

[5] Sc. not even in a man of the house of Israel have I found like this faith.

§ 34. FOXES HAVE HOLES.

A.—M. viii 18 : L. ix. 57^b : M. viii. 19, 20 : L. ix. 59-62.

E$_m$ 74.

I will come and follow thee. Foxes have their dens ; and the Son of Man has no place where he may lay his head.

✠

§ 35. STILLING THE TEMPEST.

A.—Mar. iv. 35^a : L. viii. 22^b : Mar. iv. 36^a : L. viii. 22^a : Mar. iv. 36^b : M. viii. 24^a : L. viii. 23 : Mar. iv. 38^a : M. viii. 25 : L. viii. 24^b : Mar. iv. 39^b, 40^a : L. viii. 25^b-27^a.

E$_m$ 75.

He rebuked the wind and it ceased.

✠

§ 36. THE DEMONIAC OF GADARA.

A$_c$—Mar. v. 2^b: L. viii. 27^b: Mar. v. 3^b, 4^a: L. viii. 29^b: Mar. v. 4^b,5^a: M. viii. 28^b: Mar. v. 5^b-7^a: L. viii. 28^b : Mar. v. 7^b : L. viii. 29^a-32, 35^a : Mar. v. 13^b : L. viii. 34-36 : Mar. v. 16^b : L. viii. 37 : M. ix. 1 : L. viii. 38, 39 : Mar. v. 20, 21^a.

E$_m$ 75, 76.

(Gergesenes). And the demons began to pray that he would not drive them out from this place, and send them before their time (M. viii. 29) into Gehenna.[1] (L. viii. 31). (sent the man away saying) Go, proclaim.

✠

§ 37. JAIRUS' DAUGHTER AND THE SICK WOMAN.

A$_c$—L. viii. 40^b, 41^a : Mar. v. 23^a: M. ix. 18^b, 19 : Mar. v. 24^b-30 : L. viii. 45^b-47^a : Mar. v. 33^a : L. viii. 47^b, 48 : Mar. v. 34^b : L. viii. 49-50 : Mar. v. 37-39 : L. viii. 53 : Mar. v. 40, 41 : L. viii. 55^a : Mar. v. 42^b: L. viii. 55^b, 56.

E$_m$ 76-90.

Fearing and trembling (Mar. v. 33) behind him, she touched the border of his garment. And she knew in herself that she had been cured from her torments. Who touched me ? (L.) Who touched my clothes ? (Mar.) The crowds of people surround and press thee, and sayest thou,

---

[1] Sc. to Gihanna.

Who came nigh to me ?   I know that some one has touched
me : I know that great power has gone out of me.   (When
she saw that this also had not been hidden from him.[1])
Go in peace, thy faith hath made thee whole.

Believe firmly,[2] and thy daughter shall live.   And he
commanded that they should give her something to eat.

✠

§ 38. Two Blind Men and a Dumb Demoniac.
A$_c$—M. ix. 26-33, 35, 36.

E$_m$ *No ref.*

✠

§ 39. The Mission of the Twelve.
A$_c$—M. x. 1ᵃ : L. ix. 1ᵇ, 2 : M. x. 5ᵇ-10ᵃ : Mar. vi. 8ᵇ : L. ix. 3ᵇ :
M. x. 10ᵇ : Mar. vi. 9 : M. x. 10ᶜ-14ᵃ : Mar. vi. 11ᵇ : M. x.
15-27 : L. xii. 3ᵇ. 4ᵃ : M. x. 28ᵇ : L. xii. 5ᵃ : M. x. 28ᶜ : L. xii.
5ᵇ : M. x. 29-33 : L. xii. 51-3 : M. x. 36-42 : Mar. ix. 40ᵇ :
M. xi. 1.

E$_m$ 90-8.

He sent them two by two according to His own pattern.[3]
Depart not into the way of the Gentiles . . . to the lost
sheep of the house of Israel.   Freely ye have received,
freely give.   Possess no gold . . . no staff . . . sandals.
Into whatsoever house ye enter, first salute the house.
Shake off the dust of your feet . . . it shall be more
tolerable for the land of the dwellers in Sodom.   Therefore,
behold I send you as sheep in the midst of wolves : be ye
therefore innocent as doves, and prudent as serpents.
Beware of men.   Into whatsoever town ye enter, and they
receive you not, flee thence into another town, and if from
this they persecute you, flee again into another town.
[If they have persecuted me they will also persecute you.
J. xv. 20.]   Verily I say to you, ye shall not be able to
finish these cities until I shall have come to you.   The
things which I speak to you in darkness, speak ye in the
light; what ye hear in the ear, proclaim over the housetops.
Fear not them who slay the body, but are not able to slay
the soul.   Two sparrows are sold for a farthing, and not one
of them falls to the ground without your Father.   I will

---

[1] Sc. that not even this escaped him.
[2] Sc. believing believe and thy daughter shall live.
[3] This strange reading may be due to some mistake in the original
adoption or subsequent translation of Luke x. 1.

confess him before my Father . . . I will deny him. Think
not that I came to send peace in the earth . . . a sword,
I came to separate a man from his father. [He who wishes
to find his life shall lose it, he who loses his life for my
sake shall find it. M. xvii. 25.] [He who loves not me
more than his own life. L. xiv. 26.] He who receives you
receives me.

✠

§ 40.   MARTHA AND MARY.
A*c*—L. x. 38-42.

E*m* 98.

Mary came[1] and sat at the feet of Jesus. Thou hast no
care for me,[2] tell my sister to help me. She has chosen the
good part, that for evermore it may not be taken away from
her.

✠

§ 41.   THE APOSTLES PREACH AND ANOINT THE SICK.
A*c*—Mar. vi. 12, 13.

E*m* *No ref.*

✠

§ 42.   MESSAGE OF JOHN THE BAPTIST.
A*c*—L. vii. 18 : M. xi. 2ᵃ : L. vii. 19-27 : M. xi. 11 : L. vii. 29. 30 :
M. xi. 12ᵃ : L. xvi. 16 : M. xi. 12ᵇ-15 : L. xvi. 17 : L. vii. 31ᵇ-35.

E*m* 99-108.

Art thou he who is to come, or look we for another ?
Go and tell John what ye have seen. Behold the blind see,
the lame walk, and the lepers are cleansed, and the deaf
hear, the dead arise : blessed is he who shall not have been
offended in me. He began to say to the people concerning
John : What went ye out to see in the desert ? A reed
shaken by the wind ? Or a man in soft clothing adorned ?
Such men live in king's palaces. (L. vii. 25.) He is a
prophet, yea more than a prophet. Behold I send my angel
before thee. There is no greater among the sons of women :
but he who is least in the kingdom of heaven is greater than
he. The law and the prophets until John. (M. xi. 13.)

---

[1] Sc. and she came, sat at the feet of Our Lord, etc.
[2] Sc. my Lord, dost thou not care respecting me, etc.

§ 43. A Blind and Dumb Demoniac. The Pharisees Blaspheme.

A.—Mar. iii. 20: L. xi. 14: M. xii. 24: L. xi. 16: M. xii. 25. 26ᴬ : Mar. iii. 26ᵇ : M. xii. 26ᵇ : L. xi. 18ᵇ : M. xii. 27–9 : L. xi. 21–3 : Mar. iii. 28–30 : M. xii. 32–4 : L. vi. 45ᵃ : M. xii 36–7 : L. xii. 54–5 : M. xvi. 2ᵇ–4 : M. xii. 22–3.

E_m 111–113.

They brought to him a certain man possessed with a demon, deaf and dumb and blind ;[1] he cured him and gave him hearing, speech and sight (M).

He who speaks a word concerning the Son of Man it shall be remitted him ; but he who speaks it concerning the Holy Spirit, it shall not be remitted him, neither in this world, nor in that (M). He shall be guilty of sins for eternity. (Mar. iii. 29.)

✠

§ 44. The Apostles return and announce their success. The Retreat of Christ.

A.—Mar. vi. 30, 31.

E_m *No ref.*

✠

§ 45. The Woman who was a Sinner. The two Debtors.

A.—L. vii. 36–50.

E_m 113–115.

How could this man if he were a prophet be ignorant in what manner of life this woman lived, for, you must know, she is a sinner? One creditor had two debtors, the one owed five hundred pence, and the other fifty. He said to Simon the Pharisee, I entered thy house, and thou gavest no water for my feet : one kiss of salutation thou didst not give me ; but she from the time that she entered ceased not to kiss my feet. And therefore her sins which are many have been forgiven her because she loved vehemently, because he to whom little is forgiven loves little.[2]

---

[1] Sc. then they brought near before him one man upon whom was a devil, and blind and dumb : and he healed him, and that dumb spake and saw and heard.

[2] Sc. for to whom little is forgiven, he loveth little.

§ 46. Many Believe, but Jesus will not trust Himself to them.

A*c*—J. ii. 23b-25.

E*m* *No ref.*

✠

§ 47. Mission of the Seventy. Jesus Upbraids the Unbeleiving Cities. The Seventy Return. Jesus Rejoices ; and Invites the Weary and Heavy Laden.

A*c*—L. x. 1-12 : M. xi. 20-24 : L. x. 16-22 : M. xi. 28-30.

E*m* 115-117.

He sent them two by two according to his own pattern.[1]
Freely ye have received, freely give. (M. x. 8. See § 39.)
I beheld Satan that he fell like lightning from heaven.
Behold I have given you the power of treading on serpents
and scorpions, and all the power of the enemy.

I give thee thanks, heavenly [2] Father, because thou hast
hidden these things from the wise and prudent, and hast re-
vealed them to the little ones. No one knows the Father
but the Son, and no one knows the Son but the Father.

Come unto me ye that labour and are heavy laden, and I
will refresh you. (M. xi. 28.)

✠

§ 48. On Cross-bearing. Parables of the Tower and the King.

A*c*—L. xiv. 25-33.

E*m* 118.

He who hates not his own life cannot be my disciple.
Who is there of you who, wishing to build a tower, does not
first sit down and reckon its cost ?[3]

✠

§ 49. Seeking a Sign. The Unclean Spirit's Return.

A*c*—M. xii. 38-9 : L. xi. 30 : M. xii. 40 : L. xi. 31 : M. xii. 41
L. xi. 24-6 : M. xii. 45b.

E*m* 118-122.

We wish to see a sign from thee. This generation is an
evil and adulterous generation, it seeks a sign, and no sign

---

[1] See § 39.
[2] This word "heavenly," which E found in T. here furnishes him
with an opportunity of citing "Graecus," which omits "heavenly."
[3] Sc. its costs. (But the Greek might also be rendered by "its.")

shall be given it, but the sign of Jonas the prophet : for as
Jonas was in the belly of a fish three days and three nights,
so must the Son of Man enter into the heart of the earth
three days and three nights.

And the queen of the south shall judge it.

But that impure one, if he shall have gone out of the
man. (I will return into my first house, with my seven
companions[1]). That impure one goes, takes seven others,
his companions, who are more wicked than himself, and
they come and dwell in him, and the last of that man shall
be worse than the first. Thus shall it be also to this generation.

✠

§ 50. BLESSED IS THE WOMB THAT BARE THEE.

A*c*—L. xi. 27-8.

E*m* 122, 123.

Blessed is (*v.l.*, will be) the womb that carried thee.
Blessed are they who hear the Word of God, and keep it.

✠

§ 51. HIS MOTHER AND BROTHERS.

A*c*—M. xii. 46ᵃ : L. viii. 19ᵃ : M. xii. 46ᵇ : L. viii. 19ᵇ : Mar. iii. 31ʰ : M. xii. 47-50.

E*m* 122.

Behold thy mother and thy brethren seek thee.

✠

§52. CIRCUIT OF JESUS WITH HIS DISCIPLES AND CERTAIN MINISTERING WOMEN.

A*c*—L. viii. 1-3.

E*m* 120.

Mary Magdalene, from whom he had cast out seven
demons ; and Joanna the wife of Cusa, Herod's tribune ; and
Susanna.

---

[1] Unceitain whether due to E. or T.

§ 53. TEACHING AT THE SEASHORE. THE SOWER, AND EXPLANATION.

A_c—M. xiii. 1-4ª : L. viii. 5ᵇ : M. xiii. 5, 6; L. viii. 7 : Mar. iv. 7ᵇ : I. viii. 8ª : Mar. iv. 8ᵇ : L. viii. 8ᵇ : Mar. iv. 10, 11 : M. xiii. 12-16 : L. x. 23ᵇ : M. xiii. 17 : Mar. iv. 13ʰ : M. xiii. 18: Mar. iv. 14 : M. xiii. 19-21ª : L. viii. 13ᵇ : M. xiii 21ᵇ, 22ª : Mar. iv. 19ᵇ : L. viii. 15 : M. xiii. 23ᵇ.

Eₘ 123-126,

Behold the sower went out to sow seed, and while he sowed some fell. . . . on rocky places, and other fell among thorns, and other fell into good ground. He that hath ears of hearing let him hear. That which fell near the path. And that which was over the rocky places.[1] But the good and rich soil . . . thirtyfold, and sixtyfold, and an hundredfold fruit.

✠

§ 54. THE SEED GROWING SECRETLY.

A_c—Mar. iv. 26-9.

Eₘ 126.

He knoweth not that the earth beareth fruit of herself.

✠

§ 55. THE TARES.

A_c—M. xiii. 24-30.

Eₘ 126.

Master, didst not thou sow seed of holy sowing in thy field, whence therefore the tares?

✠

§ 56. MUSTARD SEED, LEAVEN, AND SUMMARY.

A_c—M. xiii. 31ª : L. xiii. 18 : Mar. iv. 30ᵇ : L. xiii. 19ª : M. xiii. 31ᵇ : Mar. iv. 31ᵇ : M. xiii. 32ᵇ : Mar. iv. 32ᵇ, 33ª : L. xiii. 20ᵇ : M. xiii. 33ᵇ 34ª : Mar iv. 33ᵇ : M. xiii. 34ᵇ, 35 : Mar. iv. 34ᵇ.

Eₘ 127, 128.

Again the kingdom of heaven is like a grain of mustard, which is the smallest of all seeds, and if it shall germinate it increases and becomes a tree, and becomes the greatest of all herbs, and the birds of the heaven come and dwell in its branches. . . . to leaven.

---

[1] Moesinger here prints in large type the words, "If thou wishest to be perfect, go sell all that thou hast." These words are evidently only part of E.'s comment, and were not included in T.

B

§ 57.   EXPLANATION OF TARES.   PARABLES OF TREASURE,
PEARL, AND NET.

A$_c$—M. xiii. 36–53.

E$_m$ 128.

It is like a net cast into the sea and gathering of all kinds.

✠

§ 58.   TEACHING IN SYNAGOGUES.   REJECTION AT NAZA-
RETH.

A$_c$—M. xiii. 54ᵃ : Mar. vi. 2 : M. xiii. 55–7ᵃ : L. iv. 23–4 : Mar. vi. 4 :
L. iv. 25–7 : Mar. vi. 5, 6ᵃ : L. iv. 28–30 : Mar. vi. 6ᵇ.

E$_m$ 128–131.

Therefore he came into his own town, and taught them
in their synagogues. After these things he entered according
to his custom, into their synagogues, on the Sabbath day.
In Bethsaida.[1]

Physician heal thyself. A prophet is not accepted in his
own country. [The Galileans received him. J. iv. 45.]
Many widows were in the house of Israel, and to none of
them was he sent. Lepers in the house of Israel. In the
house of Israel he had not been able to do any mighty
work. (Mar. vi. 5.)

✠

§ 59.   HEROD THINKS THAT CHRIST IS JOHN RISEN FROM
THE DEAD.   ACCOUNT OF JOHN'S MARTYRDOM.

A$_c$—M. xiv. 1 : L. ix. 7ᵇ : Mar. vi. 14 : L. ix. 7ᶜ, 8ᵃ : M. xvi. 14ᵇ :
L. ix. 8ᵇ : Mar. vi. 15–6 : M. xiv. 2ᵇ : Mar. vi. 17–20 : M. xiv. 5.
Mar. vi. 21–9 : M. xiv. 12ᵇ : L. ix. 9.

E$_m$ 131, 132.

Command that the head of John the Baptist be brought.

---

[1] E. in his comment on this passage is evidently confuting an argument which Marcion had founded on it. So that Moesinger supposes
that the mistake " Bethsaida " for " Nazareth " was Marcion's, as
elsewhere in this context E. always has " Nazareth."

§ 60. CHRIST CROSSES THE LAKE. FIVE THOUSAND FED.

A$_c$—M. xiv. 13ᵃ : J. vi. 1ᵇ : Mar. vi. 33 : J. vi. 2ᵇ–5ᵃ : Mar. vi. 34ᵇ : L. ix. 11ᵇ : M. xiv. 15ᵃ : Mar. vi. 36 : M. xiv. 16. 17ᵃ : J. vi. 5ᵇ–9 : L. ix. 13 : J. vi. 10 : Mar. vi. 40 : M. xiv. 18 : Mar. vi. 41 : M. xiv. 19ᵇ, 20ᵃ : J. vi. 12, 13 : M. xiv. 21.

E$_m$ 132–134.

Gather up the fragments of the repast (that nothing of them be lost). Verily this is the prophet of whom it was said that he should come into the world (J.)

✠

§ 61. WALKING ON THE SEA.

A$_c$—Mar. vi. 45 : J. vi. 14–8 : M. xiv. 24–5 : J. vi. 19 : M. xiv. 26–33 : J. vi. 21ᵇ : Mar. vi. 54ᵃ, 51, 52, 54ᵇ–6.

E$_m$ 134–136.

And when the day was toward evening, the disciples arose and embarked on the ship (M) that they might go to Capharnaum (J), but the Lord ascended to the mountain, that he might pray (M) alone (J).

It is I, be not afraid.

When the Lord had come and with Peter had got up into the ship, the wind ceased, and calmed (M).

They came and drew nigh to the Lord, and began to adore him, and say, Verily thou art the Son of God (M).

✠

§ 62. DISCOURSE ON THE BREAD OF LIFE.

A$_c$—J. vi. 22–72.

E$_m$ 136–7.

What sign doest thou that we may see and believe in thee? Our fathers eat the manna in the desert, as it is also written, He gave them the bread of heaven to eat. No one can come to me except the Father who sent me, draw him to himself. This is the bread which came down from heaven; if anyone shall eat of this, shall he also die?[1] (*num et morietur?*) Everyone who eats of this bread shall live for ever.

---

[1] Sc. that a man may eat of it and die.

§ 63. Jesus dines with a Pharisee. On washing, and traditions generally. Every plant which my heavenly Father hath not planted shall be rooted up.

Ac—L xi. 37–41 : Mar. vii. 1–5 : M. xv. 3, 4ᴬ : Mar. vii. 10ᵇ–13, and 8, 9 : M. xv. 7–9 : Mar. vii. 14–6 : M. xv. 12–4 : Mar. vii. 17ᴬ : M. xv. 15–6ᴬ : Mar. vii. 18–9 : M. xv. 18 : Mar. vii. 21–3 : M. xv. 20ᵇ.

Eₘ 137, 138.

God said, Honour thy father and thy mother . . . he who curses his father or his mother let him die by death (M). And ye say to each[1] one of your fathers and your mothers, Come now, that wherewith thou mightest have been profited by me, is a gift.

Every planting which my heavenly Father has not planted shall be plucked up by the roots.

✠

§ 64. The Syrophœnician Woman.

Ac—M. xv. 21ᴬ : Mar. vii. 24ᵇ–6 : M. xv. 22–8ᴬ : Mar. vii. 29ᵇ : M. xv. 28ᵇ : Mar. vii. 30.

Eₘ 138, 139.

A woman called out and followed him, saying, Have mercy on me. But he gave her no answer. It is not good to take the bread of sons and cast[2] it forth to dogs. Yea Lord even the dogs eat of the crumbs of their master's[3] table. I say to thee, woman, great is thy faith.

✠

§ 65. A Deaf Mute at Decapolis.

Ac—Mar. vii. 31–7.

Eₘ *No ref.*

---

[1] Sc. But ye say, each to his father and his mother.
[2] Moesinger's Latin gives "proficere," but I fancy this must be a printer's error for "projicere." The latter reading is adopted by Zahn, who does not make any comment on it.
[3] "master's" here in the singular seems to be unique.

§ 66. The Woman of Samaria.

A$_c$—J. iv. 4-45^a.

E$_m$ 140-143.

Give me a drink of water.   The woman says to him,
Behold thou art[1] a Jew.   He says to her, If thou knewest
him who said to thee, Give me of this water to drink, thou
wouldst have asked of him.   The woman says to him,
Thou hast no pitcher, and the well is deep.   (He says to
her, my water comes down from heaven.)[2]   He who drinks
of this water, which I shall give him, shall never thirst.
The woman says to him, Lord give me of that water, that
I thirst not, nor come another time to this well, to draw
water from it.   He says to her, Go call me thy husband.
Thou hast changed five husbands, and he whom thou now
hast is not thy husband.   The woman says to him, Lord it
seems to me that thou art a prophet.   Our fathers
worshipped in this mountain.   He answers her, Verily I say
to thee, neither in this mountain, nor in Jerusalem, shall
they worship, but the true worshippers shall worship in spirit
and in truth.   Behold the Christ cometh, and when he
shall have come, he shall give us all things.   He says to her,
I who speak with thee am he.   They wondered that he was
talking with a woman.   Not henceforth on account of thy
words do we believe in him, but because we have heard his
teaching, and seen his works, that he is God, and we have
recognized that he is surely the very Christ.

✠

§ 67. The Leper.   Many Cures.

A$_c$—L. v. 12 : Mar. i. 41-5 : L. v. 15^b, 16.

E$_m$ 143-145.

Lord, if thou wilt thou canst cure me.   And he stretched
out his hand.   Tell no man: go show thyself to the
priests, and offer the gift, (as Moses commanded you) to
testify to them.   (*Lat.—on account of their testimony.*)

---

[1] Sc. Lo thou art a Jew.
[2] Not in large type in Moesinger's Latin ; but from the way in which
E. quotes it, we conclude that it may have been in T.

§ 68. The Impotent Man at Bethesda.   Discourse.

Aₑ—J. v. 1-47.

Eₘ 145-152.

[1] There was a certain man there who had an infirmity thirty-eight years.   The Lord says to him, Dost thou wish to be made whole?   The infirm man says to him, I have no helper, that if the waters are moved he may send me down, and while I move myself slowly, already another goes down before me.   Arise (*v.l.* stand on thy feet), take up thy bed, and walk to thy house.[2]   Who commanded thee to take up thy bed on thee on the Sabbath day?   He who cured me said to me, Arise, take up thy bed and walk.   They said to him, Who is he?   He said, I know not.   Because Jesus, when he saw the multitude of people,[3] turned aside from that place.   And after some time he saw him and said to him, Behold thou art made whole, henceforth sin no more, lest thou have need of some one else.[4]   And then the man went away and related to the Jews that Jesus was he who made me whole.[5]

My Father works his work even until to-day,[6] therefore also I work.   They persecuted him . . . but also because he called God his own father, and made himself equal with God.   The Father judges no one, but has given all judgment into the hands of his Son.   As the Father has life in himself, so also has he given to the Son.   He has given him power that the Son of Man should execute judgment. Nor from men do I receive any witness.   He is the lamp which was shining.   Because I have witness which is greater than that of John.   The very works which I do bear witness of me.   Moses himself is your accuser : Moses wrote of me.

✠

§ 69. Cures at Sea of Galilee.   Four Thousand Fed.

Aₑ—M. xv. 29, 30ᵃ: J. iv. 45ᵇ: M. xv. 30ᵇ-32 : Mar. viii. 3ᵇ: M. xv. 33-39.

Eₘ *No ref.*

---

[1] F. plainly shows by his comments that he had before him the verses about the angel, which are also in A., and most probably were in the original T.

[2] Sc. Rise, take up thy bed and walk, go to thy house.

[3] Sc. on account of the multitude of men.

[4] Zahn thinks this represents a reading ἵνα μὴ χρεία σοί τινος γένηται, for ἵνα μὴ χεῖρον σοί τι γένηται.

[5] Sc. Jesus it is that hath made me whole.

[6] Sc. My Father until now doeth works, on this account also I too work.

§ 70. A Sign again Sought. The Leaven of the Pharisees and Sadducees.

A_c—M. xvi. 1ᵃ: Mar. viii. 11ᵇ, 12ᵃ : M. xvi. 4ᵇ : Mar. viii. 12ᵇ–15 :
M. xvi. 7, 8ᵃ : Mar. viii. 17ᵇ–21ᵃ : M. xvi. 11, 12.

E_m *No ref.*

✠

§ 71. The Blind Man at Bethsaida.

A_c—Mar. viii. 22–26.

E_m 153.

He saw all things clearly.

✠

§ 72. At Cæsarea Philippi. Peter's Confession.

A_c—Mar. viii. 27 : M. xvi. 13–20.

E_m 153, 154.

What do men say of me, that the Son of Man is?[1]   They
answer him, Some say that he is Elias, others that he is
Jeremias.   But ye, what say ye of me that I am?   Simon
said, Thou art the Christ, the Son of the living God.   And
he answered, Blessed art thou, Simon.   Thou art a rock,
and the gates of Hades (*portae inferi*) shall not conquer
thee.   Tell no one of me that I am the Christ.

✠

§ 73. Christ foretells His Sufferings. Peter Rebuked. What shall a Man give in Exchange for his Soul?

A_c—M. xvi. 21ᵃ : Mar. viii. 31ᵇ, 32ᵃ : M. xvi. 22 : Mar. viii. 33ᵃ :
M. xvi. 23ᵇ : Mar. viii. 34ᵃ: L. ix. 23ᵇ : Mar. viii. 35 : L. ix. 25 :
Mar. viii. 37, 38 : M. xvi. 27.

E_m 154, 155.

Behold we go up to Jerusalem, and all things are being
fulfilled which have been written of me ; that the Son of
Man must be crucified and die.   Far be it from thee Lord,
that thou shouldst do this.   He answered him, Get thee
behind me Satan, (for thou art an offence to me), for thou
thinkest not the things which are of God, but the things
which are of man.

---

[1] Sc, What say men concerning me that I am?   Who forsooth is this
Son of Man?

§ 74. TRANSFIGURATION.

A*c*—Mar. viii. 39: M. xvi. 28ᵇ, xvii. 1: L. ix. 29ᴬ: M. xvii. 2ᵇ:
L. ix. 29ᵇ: Mar. ix.2ᵇ, 3: L. ix. 31ᵇ–33ᵃ: M. xvii. 4ᵇ: L. ix. 33ᵇ:
Mar. ix. 5ᵇ: M. xvii. 5ᵃ: L. ix. 34ᵇ: M. xvii. 5ᵇ: L. ix. 36ᴬ:
M. xvii. 6–9: Mar. ix. 9ᵃ: L. ix. 36ᵇ: Mar. ix .9ᵇ, 10ᴬ: M. xvii.
10ᵇ: Mar. ix. 11, 12: M. xvii. 12ᵇ, 13.

E*m* 155–159.

There will be some who are now standing here with me,
who shall not taste of death. If thou wilt Lord, let us
make here three tabernacles. He knew not what he was
saying. This is my beloved Son, hear him and ye shall
live. And while they were coming down from the mountain,
he gave them a command and said, Take heed that ye tell
no one this vision which ye have seen (until the Son of Man
rise from the dead).

✠

§ 75. ON HIS DESCENT FROM THE MOUNT A CROWD RUNS TO MEET HIM. THE PHARISEES TELL HIM OF HEROD'S THREAT.

A*c*—Mar. ix. 13, 14: L. xiii. 31–33.

E*m* 159.

It must not be that a prophet perish out of Jerusalem.

✠

§ 76. DEMONIAC BOY. SUFFERINGS AGAIN FORETOLD. DISCIPLES DISPUTE WHICH OF THEM WILL BE GREATEST.

A*c*—L. ix. 38ᵃ: M. xvii. 14ᵇ: L. ix. 38ᵇ, 39ᵃ: M. xvii. 14ᵇ: Mar.
ix. 17: M. xvii. 14ᶜ: L. ix. 39ᵇ: M. xvii. 15. 16: Mar. ix. 19,
20, and 21ᵇ–26ᵃ: L. ix. 43ᵇ: M. xvii. 17ᵇ: L. ix. 44ᴬ: Mar. ix.
27: M. xvii. 19: Mar. ix. 28–30ᵃ: L. ix. 44ᵇ: Mar. ix. 30ᵇ:
L. ix. 45: M. xvii. 22ᵇ: L. ix. 46: Mar. ix. 32, 33.

E*m* 160, 161.

They were not able to cure him. O generation evil,[1]
perverse, and unbelieving, how long shall I be with you?
To him who believes are all things possible. I say to thee,
unclean, deaf, and dumb one, go out, depart from him, and
enter no more into him. Why were not we able to cure
him? On account of your unbelief.

---

[1] Sc. O race, perverse and without faith.

§ 77. THE STATER IN THE FISH'S MOUTH.

A_c—M. xvii. 23^b-26.

E_m 161.

The kings of the earth, from whom take they tribute ? From sons or from foreigners? That to these men thou mayest give no offence, go to the sea, and cast there a net.

✠

§ 78. JESUS BEING ASKED WHO IS GREATEST IN THE KINGDOM OF HEAVEN, MAKES A LITTLE CHILD THE MEANS OF CONVEYING SPIRITUAL IN- STRUCTION.

A_c—M. xviii. 1 : L. ix. 47^a : Mar ix. 35 : M. xviii. 3 : L. ix. 48^a : Mar. ix. 36^b : L. ix. 48^b : M. xviii. 6.

E_m *No ref.*

✠

§ 79. THOSE MUST NOT BE PREVENTED WHO DO GOOD IN THE NAME OF JESUS. ON OFFENCES.

A_c—L. ix. 49 : Mar. ix. 38 : L. ix. 50^b : M. xviii. 7, 8 : Mar. ix. 43 : M. xviii. 9^a : Mar. ix. 46^b-49^a : L. xiv. 34^b, 35 : Mar. ix. 49^b.

E_m *No ref.*

✠

§ 80. ON DIVORCE.

A_c—Mar. x. 1-5^a : M. xix. 4^b-9^a : Mar. x. 10-12 : M. xix. 9^b-12.

E_m 162.

They came and drew nigh that they might ask him, Is it lawful for anyone to put away his wife ? Moses on account of the hardness of your heart gave you permission, but from the beginning of the creation this was not.

✠

§ 81. SUFFER THE LITTLE CHILDREN TO COME UNTO ME.

A_c—M. xix. 13^a : Mar. x. 13^b-16.

E_m *No ref.*

§ 82.   PARABLES OF THE LOST SHEEP, AND LOST PIECE OF SILVER.

A.—L. xv. 1–4 :   M. xviii.   13^b :   L.   xv.   5^b, 6 :   M. xviii.   14 :
L. xv. 7–10.

E. 162.

[1] TEN DRACHMAE AND A HUNDRED SHEEP.

✠

§ 83.   THE PRODIGAL SON.

A$_c$—L. xv. 11–32.

E. 163.

And when the younger son had squandered his goods.
It behoved us to rejoice, because thy brother was dead, and
lives, and has been recalled to life.

✠

§ 84.   UNJUST STEWARD.

A$_c$—L. xvi. 1–12.

E. 163.

[2] CONCERNING A STEWARD.

✠

§ 85.   THE UNMERCIFUL SERVANT.   A SINNING BROTHER. PETER'S QUESTION.

A.—M. xviii. 23–35 :   L. xvii. 3, 4 :   M. xviii. 15–22.

E. 163–165.

How often if my brother sin against me shall I forgive
him ?   Till seven times, is it enough ?   He says to him,
Until seventy-seven times seven.[3]
Where one is there also am I, and where two are there
also will I be.

---

[1] These words are printed in the usual large type in Moesinger's Ed.
They evidently form a title, which E. had before him, and which was
probably in T.
[2] See note on § 82.
[3] Sc. He saith to him, Not seven : but above seventy-seven seven.

§ 86.   RESPONSIBILITY OF KNOWING GOD'S WILL.   TAKE
HEED THAT YE DESPISE NOT ONE OF THESE
LITTLE ONES.

A$_c$—L. xii. 47–50 : M. xviii. 10, 11.

E$_n$ 165.

Their angels in the heavens behold the face of my Father.

✠

§ 87.   THE SLAIN GALILEANS.   THE TOWER IN SILOAM.
PARABLE OF THE FIG TREE.

A$_c$—J. vii. 1 : L. xiii. 1–9.

E$_n$ 165, 166.

Mixed their blood with their sacrifices.   A certain man
had planted in his vineyard a fig tree, and says to the
husbandman, There are these three years that I come to
seek fruit of this fig tree, cut it down.   The husbandman
answered and said to him, Leave it alone this year also.

✠

§ 88.   WOMAN WITH SPIRIT OF INFIRMITY.

A$_c$—L. xiii. 10–17.

E$_n$ *No ref.*

✠

§ 89.   JESUS GOES TO THE FEAST OF TABERNACLES.

A$_c$—J. vii. 2–10^a : M. xix. 1^b, 2 : J. vii. 10^b–31.

E$_n$ 167. 168.

They say to him, There is no one who does any work in
secret.   For his brothers did not believe in him.   I go not
up in this feast.   Why seek ye to slay me, a man who tells
the truth ?

✠

§ 90.   THE RICH FOOL.

A$_c$—L. xii. 13–21.

E$_n$ *No ref.*

§ 91. The Young Ruler. The Reward of those who leave all for Christ.

Ac—Mar. x. 17-19ᵃ: M. xix. 17ᵇ, 18ᵃ: Mar. x. 19ᵇ: M. xix. 19ᵇ, 20 : Mar. x. 21ᵃ: M. xix. 21ᵇ, 22ᵃ: L. xviii. 23ᵇ, 24ᵃ: Mar. x. 23 : M. xix. 23ᵇ, 24 : Mar. x. 24-27: L. xviii. 28 : M. xix. 27ᵇ, 28 : Mar. x. 29ᵇ: L. xviii. 30 : Mar. x. 30ᵇ, 31.

E., 168-174.

Good Master, what shall I do that I may live? Why callest thou me good? No one is good, except only one, God the Father who is in heaven. If thou wishest to enter into eternal life keep the Commandments. Dost thou know the Commandments? What lack I yet? Thou hast still need of another thing. [Do this and thou shalt live. Luke x. 28.] How hard it is for those who trust in possessions.

✠

§ 92. Dives and Lazarus.

A*c*—L. xvi. 14-31.

E., 174, 175.

[1] Of the Rich Man and Lazarus.

My son remember that thou in thy life receivedst thy good things, and Lazarus his torments.
If they hear not Moses and the prophets.

✠

§ 93. The Labourers in the Vineyard.

A*c*—M. xx. 1-16.

E., 175-177.

[1] Of the Labourers, whom the Master of the Vineyard had hired at the Third, the Sixth, and the Ninth hour.

Why do ye stand idle all day to the evening? No one came and hired us. Or have I not the power in mine own house of doing what I wish? If I am liberal, why is your eye evil?

---

[1] See note on § 82.

§ 94. IN THE HOUSE OF ONE OF THE CHIEF PHARISEES ON
THE SABBATH. A MAN WITH DROPSY. CHIEF
SEATS AT FEASTS. INVITE THE POOR AND
INFIRM.

A$_c$—L. xiv. 1–15.

E$_m$ *No ref.*

✠

§ 95. THE MARRIAGE OF THE KING'S SON AND THE
GREAT SUPPER.

A$_c$—M. xxii. 1, 2 : L. xiv. 16ᵇ, 17: M. xxii. 3ᵇ: L. xiv. 18–20 :
M. xxii. 4–6 : L. xiv. 21ᵃ: M. xxii. 7, 8 : L. xiv 21ᵇ–23ᵃ: M.
xxii. 9ᵇ: L. xiv. 23ᵇ, 24: M. xxii. 10–14.

E$_m$ *No ref.*

✠

§ 96. JESUS GOING UP TO JERUSALEM CLEANSES TEN
LEPERS.

A$_c$—J. v. 1: L. xvii. 11–19.

E$_m$ *No ref.*

✠

§ 97. JESUS AGAIN FORETELLS HIS SUFFERINGS. AMBI-
TIOUS REQUEST OF JAMES AND JOHN.

A$_c$—Mar. x. 32 : L. xviii. 31ᵇ: Mar. x. 33, 34ᵃ: L. xviii. 33, 34 :
M. xx. 20, 21ᵃ: Mar. x. 35–44: M. xx. 28.

E$_m$ 177–179.

We wish that whatsoever we shall ask thou mayest do
for us. (I will do it for you.[1]) Give us authority that one
of us may sit at thy right hand, and the other at thy left
hand. Are ye able to drink of the cup which I am about to
drink ?

---

[1] Sc. is wanting here, but D. Itt., which usually agree with it, support this reading of T.

§ 98. Are there few that be saved?

A*c*—L. xiii. 22–30.

E*m*   *No ref.*

✠

§ 99. Zacchaeus.

A*c*— L. xix. 1–10.

E*m* 180.

Zacchaeus make haste, come down from that. Behold, Lord, the half of all my goods I will give to the poor, and all[1] things which I have ever unjustly accepted from anyone, I will restore these fourfold. To-day has salvation been accomplished for this house, for even he also is a son of Abraham.

✠

§ 100. Bartimaeus.

A*c* —L. xviii. 35[a] : M. xx. 29[b] : L. xviii. 35[b] : Mar. x. 46 : L. xviii. 36, 37 : Mar. x. 47[a] : L. xviii. 38, 39 : Mar. x. 48[b]–51 : M. xx. 34[a] : L. xviii. 42[b], 43 :

E*m* 180, 181.

A certain blind man was sitting by the wayside [at the crossing of the ways. M. xxii. 9], and his name was Bartimaeus, the son of Timaeus. Jesus, Son of David, have mercy on me. They kept chiding and hindering this blind man, that he should not come to Jesus, therefore he kept calling out the more. And casting away his cloak he came to him. Receive thy sight; thy faith hath made thee whole.

✠

§ 101. Parable of the Pounds.

A*c*—L. xix. 11[b]–27.

E*m*   *No ref.*

✠

§ 102. Cleansing of the Temple.

A*c*—M. xxi. 12[a] : J. ii. 14[a] : M. xxi. 12[b] : J. ii. 14[b], 16 : M. xxi. 12[c],13 : J. ii. 16 : Mar. xi. 16 : J. ii. 17–22.

E*m* 181.

Were selling sheep and oxen in the temple.

---

[1] Sc. and every one that I have injured I recompense fourfold.

§ 103. Casting Gifts into the Treasury.

A𝒸—Mar. xii. 41, 42ᵃ : L. xxi. 3 : Mar. xii. 44.

E𝑚 *No ref.*

✠

§ 104. Parable of Pharisee and Publican.

A𝒸— L. xviii. 9–14.

E𝑚 181, 182.

[1] Of the Pharisee who was praying. (But the publican.)

✠

§ 105. Jesus lodges at Bethany. The Barren Fig-tree Cursed.

A𝒸—Mar. xi. 19ᵃ : M. xxi. 17 : L. ix. 11 : Mar. xi. 12–15ᵃ.

E𝑚 182 and 186.

He became hungry and hastily[2] came to that fig-tree. He cursed the fig-tree.

✠

§ 106. Nicodemus comes to Jesus by Night.

A𝒸—J. iii. 1–21.

E𝑚 187–189.

Can it by any means come to pass that a man when he is old should enter again into his mother's womb and again be born? (*Lat. denuo in lucem edatur ?*) Unless a man shall have been born of water and the Spirit, he cannot enter into the kingdom of God. He who is born of the flesh is flesh, and he who is born of the Spirit is spirit. Ye know not the Spirit, whence it comes or whither it goes. Art thou a Master in Israel, and knowest not these things? Therefore if I have told you earthly things, and ye have not believed, how shall ye believe if I shall tell you heavenly things (*v.l.* of heaven). And no one has ascended into heaven, but he who descended from heaven, the Son of Man.[3] And as Moses lifted up the serpent in the desert, so must the Son of Man be lifted up.

---

[1] See note on § 82.   [2] Source unknown.
[3] T. does not appear to have read the words, " which is in heaven," so commonly found as the conclusion of this verse. They are wanting also in some of the very best Gk. MSS. (N. B. L. 33.)
Sc. " which was in heaven."
Pesh. " which is in heaven."

§ 107. The Disciples wonder that the Fig-tree has so suddenly withered. On Faith and Believing Prayer.

A$_c$—Mar. xi. 19, 20 : M. xxi. 20^b : Mar. xi. 21-23 : M. xxi. 21^b, 22 : L. xvii. 5-10 : Mar. xi. 24-26.

D$_m$ 184-186.

When they returned they say to him, Behold, the fig-tree which thou cursedst how suddenly it is dried up ! (Mar.) His disciples wondered how it was dried up so suddenly. He says to them, And you, if you had faith and did not doubt (M.) in your heart (Mar.) might say to this mountain, Go, remove into the sea, and it would be transferred.

✠

§ 108. The Judge and the Widow.

A$_c$—L. xviii. 1-8.

E$_m$ 190.

[1] In this Sinful Judge.

✠

§ 109. Jesus is asked, "By what Authority doest Thou these Things?" The Parable of the Two Sons.

A$_c$—Mar. xi. 15^a : L. xx. 1, 2^a : Mar. xi. 28^b, 29^a : M. xxi. 24^b, 25^a : Mar. xi. 30^b : M. xxi. 25^b, 26 : L. xx. 6^b : Mar. xi. 32^b, 33 : M. xxi. 28-32.

E$_m$ 191, 192.

They came and said to him, By what authority doest thou these things ? The baptism of John whence was it ? Was it from heaven, or from men ? They began to deliberate with themselves, and to say, If we say that it is from heaven, he will say to us, Why did ye not believe him ? But if we say, From men ; we fear this people.

What think ye ? A certain man had two sons. Very well, sir. Which of these did the will of his father ? The second.[2] Therefore the publicans and fornicators go before you into the kingdom of the heavens. John came to you in the way of righteousness.

---

[1] See note on § 82.   [2] Against Sc., and Arabic.

§ 110. THE WICKED HUSBANDMEN.

A.—M. xxi. 33ª . L. xx. 9 : M. xxi. 34 : Mar. xii. 3–5ª : M. xxi. 35, 36 :
 L. xx. 13 : Mar. xii. 6ª : M. xxi. 38ª : L. xx. 14ᵇ : M. xxi.
 39–42ª : L. xx. 17ᵇ : M. xxi. 42ᵇ–46.

E. 192, 193.

A certain householder planted for himself a vineyard, and
sent his servants that they might bring him the fruit.   This
is the heir of this vineyard, come let us kill him, and then
the inheritance of the vineyard will be ours.   What do those
husbandmen deserve?   He will destroy the evil men by
evils.   Have ye never read, "The stone which the builders
have rejected, has itself become the head of the corner"?
Whosoever strikes against it shall be broken, and over
whomsoever it shall fall, it shall grind and consume him.

✠

§ 111. CRAFTY QUESTION ABOUT TRIBUTE.

A.—M. xxii. 15 : L. xx. 20ᵇ : M. xxii. 16, 17 : Mar. xii. 14ᵇ, 15 :
 M. xxii. 18ᵇ–21 : L. xx. 26.

E. 193.

They sent to him their disciples with the Herodians
Are they to pay tribute?   Give to Cæsar that which is
Cæsar's, but restore to God what ye owe to him.

✠

§ 112. QUESTION ABOUT MARRIAGE AT THE RESUR-
RECTION.

A.—M. xxii. 23–25ª : L. xx. 29ᵇ–31 : M. xxii. 27–29ª : Mar. xii. 24ᵇ :
 L. xx. 34ᵇ–36 : M. xxii. 30ª : Mar. xii. 26ᵇ : L. xx. 38 : Mar.
 xii. 27ᵇ : M. xxii. 33.

E. 193, 194.

The Sadducees came, and they say to him, There is no
resurrection of the dead.[1]   The patriarch [2] Moses gave us
the command, If any man die without children, let his
brother marry his wife.   Therefore a certain wife had seven
husbands.   In the resurrection therefore of the dead, whose
of these shall she be?   Ye err greatly (Mar.): for the full-

---

[1] Sc. On that day came near before him the Sadducees, and say to
him, that there is no resurrection.

[2] Aucher translates the Armenian word thus; Moesinger translates
"*praeceptor.*"

grown sons of this world marry; but those who have been
made worthy of that world, are as the angels. (L.)

✠

§ 113. QUESTION AS TO WHICH OF THE COMMANDMENTS IS
GREATEST. PARABLE OF THE GOOD SAMARITAN.

A𝑐—L. xx. 39 : M. xxii. 34, 35ᵃ: Mar. xii. 28ᵃ: L. x. 25 : Mar. xii.
28ᵇ–30ᵃ: M. xxii. 37ᵇ, 38 : Mar. xii. 31 : M. xxii. 40 : Mar. xii.
32–34 : L. x. 28–37 : Mar. xii 34ᵇ.

E. 194, 195.

What commandment is first and great in the law?[1] That
thou shouldst love the Lord thy God, and thy neighbour as
thyself.   (Who is my neighbour?)

THAT WOUNDED ONE.[2]

From Jerusalem to Jericho.   Which of these seems to
thee to have been neighbour to the wounded man? (He
says to him) He who showed mercy.   And do thou like-
wise.

✠

§ 114. CONTRAST BETWEEN UNBELIEF OF THE ECCLESI-
ASTICS, AND BELIEF OF MANY OF THE PEOPLE.
THE LAST DAY OF THE FEAST OF TABERNACLES.

A𝑐—L. xix. 47, 48 : J. vii. 31–52.

E. 196.

The Lord cried out and said, If any of you thirst, let him
come unto me and drink.

✠

§ 115.   WHAT SAY YE OF THE MESSIAH?

A𝑐—M. xxii. 41–46.

E. *No ref.*

✠

§ 116. JESUS TEACHES "I AM THE LIGHT OF THE WORLD."

Aᶜ—J. viii. 12–59.

E. 196, 197.

If ye are the sons of Abraham, do the works of Abraham.

---

[1] Sc. Which commandment is great and first in the law?
[2] See note on § 82.

Why do ye seek to kill me? Abraham did not that. Ye are the sons of Satan; (who was a manslayer from the beginning). Thou art a Samaritan, who wishes to kill thee?

Abraham desired to see my day, he saw it and rejoiced. Thou art not fifty years old, and hast thou seen Abraham? He answered them, Before Abraham was I already existed (*Antequam Abraham erat ego jam fui*).

✠

§ 117. The Man Born Blind, and Christ's Discourse about Blind Guides.

A_c—J. ix, x.

E_m 197–200.

He met a man who was blind from his mother's womb. And his disciples asked him, Whose is the sin? And he answered them, Neither this man's nor his relations'; but that the works of God may be manifested in him. And I must work the works of my Father who sent me, while it is day. And when he had said these things, he spat upon the ground and made clay of his spittle. Go wash thy face. He made this clay on the Sabbath. They who see shall become blind.

All who came before me were thieves and robbers.

✠

§ 118. Lazarus Raised. Conspiracy of the Priestly Party.

A_c—J. xi. 1–53.

E_m 200–205.

And there was a certain sick man there: Lazarus was his name: and his sisters sent to the Lord saying, Lord, behold he whom thou lovest is lying sick in bed. This disease is not unto death, but for the sake of God's glory, that the Son of Man may be glorified in him. He remained in that place where he was for two days. (And he said to his disciples) Come let us go into Judaea. (They answered him), The Jews seek to slay thee, and dost thou depart thither again? Are there not twelve hours of the day? If anyone walk in the light he stumbleth not, because he seeth the light. Lazarus our friend[1] is dead, and I am glad for your sake. Come let us go that we also may die with him. Lord if thou hadst been here. I verily am the resurrection, and the life ; whosoever believeth in me, even if he have died, he lives: he who lives and believes in me shall not die for eternity. He was troubled. (Where have ye laid him ?) And the Lord wept. Did not this man open the eyes of a blind man ? Could he not have caused that this man should not have died ? Go and take away the stone. Already he stinketh.

And if we allow him, all men will believe in him, and afterwards the Romans will come and take away our nation, the law, and this place.

✠

§ 119. Jesus Retreats to Ephraim. On his Journey to the Passover is refused Hospitality at a Samaritan Village.

Ac—J. xi. 54–56 : L. ix. 51–56.

En *No ref.*

✠

§ 120. At the House of Simon the Leper, Mary anoints the Head and Feet of Jesus.

Ac—J. xii. 1, 2 : Mar. xiv. 3ª : J. xii. 9–11, 3ª : Mar. xiv. 3ᵇ : J. xii. 3ᵇ–6 : Mar. xiv. 4 : M. xxvi. 9 : Mar. xiv. 5ᵇ : M. xxvi. 10ª : Mar. xiv. 6ᵇ : J. xii. 7ᵇ, 8ª : Mar. xiv. 7ᵇ : M. xxvi. 12 : Mar. xiv. 8ᵇ, 9.

En 205.

Simon the leper. This ointment could have been sold for three hundred pence, and given to the poor. And the chief priests took counsel to slay Lazarus also.

---

[1] "Our friend" after Lazarus is found also in D. which often agrees with Sc. Sc. wanting here.

§ 121. THE TWO DISCIPLES BORROW AN ASS AND COLT.
JESUS RIDES TOWARDS JERUSALEM AMID THE
ACCLAMATIONS OF THE MULTITUDE. HIS
LAMENT. THE WHOLE CITY MOVED.

A$_c$—L. xix. 28, 29^a : M. xxi. 1^b, 2^a : Mar. xi. 2 : M. xxi. 2^b : L. xix.
30^b : M. xxi. 2^c : L. xix. 31^a : M. xxi. 3^b-5 : J. xii. 16 :
M. xxi. 6^a : L. xix. 32^b : M. xxi. 6^b : L. xix. 33, 34^a : Mar.
xi. 6^b : M. xxi. 7, 8. L. xix. 37 : M. xxi. 9^b : Mar. xi. 10^b :
L. xix. 38^b : J. xii. 12, 13 : L. xix. 39-44 : M. xxi. 10, 11 :
J. xii. 17, 18.

E$_m$ 207, 208.

Loose the ass and bring him to me. (And when he came
to Jerusalem, seeing it he began to weep over it.) If thou
hadst known at least this day of thy peace, but peace is
hidden from thy face.[1] (The children were calling out and
saying) Blessing to the Son of David. But the chief priests
and scribes said angrily, Dost thou not hear what these
say? Rebuke the people that they keep silent altogether.[2]
He answers, If these shall keep silent, the stones at any rate
shall cry out.

✠

§ 122. ENVY OF THE CHIEF PRIESTS AND PHARISEES.
ENQUIRY OF THE GREEKS. THE VOICE FROM
HEAVEN.

A$_c$—M. xxi. 14-16 : J. xii. 1ς-36^a.

E$_m$ 208, 209.

Now is the judgment of the world, now also the Prince of
this world is cast out. We have heard in the law, that the
Christ liveth for ever, but thou sayest, The Son of Man must
be lifted up.

✠

§ 123. THE PHARISEES ENQUIRE WHEN THE KINGDOM OF
GOD SHALL COME.

A$_ĉ$—L. xvii. 20, 21.

E$_m$ 209-211.

The Kingdom of God is in your[3] heart. If they shall
say to you, Behold he is here, believe it not. As the
lightning which shineth. (L. xvii. 24.)

---

[1] Sc. But even if in this day thou hadst known thy peace! But
peace has hidden itself from thine eyes.
[2] Sc. Our Master rebuke them that they shout not. Pesh.—"thy
disciples."
[3] trans. of ἐντὸς ὑμῶν.

§ 124. Christ speaks to the Multitude and to his Disciples, concerning the Scribes and Pharisees. O Jerusalem, Jerusalem !

Ac—L. xxi. 37-8 : M. xxiii. 1-5ᵃ : Mar. xii. 37ᵇ-39 : M. xxiii. 5ᵇ, 7ᵇ : Mar. xii. 40 : M. xxiii. 8-12 : L. xi. 43 : M. xxiii. 14, 13ᵃ : L. xi. 52ᵃ : M. xxiii. 13ᵇ, 15-28 : L. xi. 45, 46 : M. xxiii. 29ᵃ : L. xi. 47ᵇ : M. xxiii. 29ᵇ-39.

E. 211-213.

Woe[1] unto you lawyers who have hidden the keys. . . . Shall come all the blood of the just ; from the blood of Abel the just, even to the blood of Zacharias . . . between the temple and the altar.

How often I wished to gather you together.

✠

§ 125. Secret Believers. Christ's Words shall Judge Unbelievers in the Last Day.

Ac—J. xii. 42-50.

E. 213.

If anyone has heard my words, and has not kept them, I have not known him. I have not come into this world to judge the world, but to save the world. He who receiveth not my words, the word which I have spoken judges him.

✠

§ 126. The Scribes and Pharisees seek to entrap Christ. He warns his Disciples against their Hypocrisy. Fulfilment of a Prophecy in the 6th Chapter of Isaiah.

Ac—L. xi. 53-xii. 3 : J. xii. 36ᵇ-41.

E. No ref.

✠

§ 127. The Disciples point out to Jesus the structure of the Temple.

Ac—M. xxiv. 1: Mar xiii. 1ᵇ : L. xxi. 5ᵇ : M. xxiv. 2ᵃ : L. xix. 43ᵇ, 44ᵇ.

E. No. ref.

---

[1] Sc. Woe to you Scribes! because ye have hidden the keys of knowledge.

§ 128. THE CHIEF PRIESTS AND SCRIBES PLOT AGAINST HIM, TWO DAYS BEFORE THE PASSOVER.

A₍ₑ₎--Mar. xiv. 1, 2.

E₍ₐ₎ *No ref.*

✠

§ 129. CHRIST ON THE MOUNT OF OLIVES SPEAKS OF THE FALL OF JERUSALEM, AND THE END OF THE WORLD.

A₍ₑ₎—Mar. xiii. 3 : L. xxi. 7ᵇ : M. xxiv. 3ᵇ, 4ᵃ : L. xvii. 22ᵇ : M. xxiv. 4ᵇ, 5 : L. xxi. 8¹ : Mar. xiii. 6ᶜ : L. xxi. 8ᶜ : Mar. xiii. 7ᵃ : M. xxiv. 6ᵇ : L. xxi. 9ᵇ : M. xxiv. 7ᵃ : L. xxi. 11 : M. xxiv. 8 : L. xxi. 12, 13 : Mar. xiii. 10 : L. xii. 11 : Mar. xiii. 11ᵇ : L. xxi. 14, 15 : M. xxiv. 9, 10 : L. xxi. 16, 18, 19 : M. xxiv. 11-14 : L. xxi. 20-22 : M. xxiv. 15, 16 : Mar. xiii. 15, 16 : L. xxi. 23, 24 : Mar. xiii. 21 : M. xxiv. 24 : Mar. xiii. 23 : M. xxiv. 26, 27 : L. xvii. 25 : M. xxiv. 20, 21 : Mar. xiii. 20 : L. xxi. 25, 26ᵃ : Mar. xiii. 24ᵃ : M. xxiv. 29-31 : L. xxi. 28 : M. xxiv. 32-35 : L. xxi. 34-36 : Mar. xiii. 32-37 : M. xxiv. 37-39 : L. xvii. 28-37 : M. xxiv. 42-44.

E₍ₘ₎ 213-218.

When ye shall see the sign of the terror of this desolation which has been mentioned by the prophet Daniel. He who stands on the housetop. Woe to them that are with child. There will be suffering for this people. Pray and ask that your flight may not be in the winter, nor on the Sabbath day. Pray that ye may be worthy to be taken away from all these things which are about to come. (L. xxi. 36.) And if God had not shortened those days no flesh would be saved. (Mar.). That day (*v.l.* that moment) no one knows, neither the Angels, nor the Son. Two shall be in the field . . . in one bed. The eagles.

✠

§ 130. THE FAITHFUL AND UNFAITHFUL STEWARDS.

A₍ₑ₎—L. xii. 41, 42ᵃ : M. xxiv. 45, 46 : L. xii. 44ᵃ : M. xxiv. 47ᵇ, 48 : L. xii. 45ᵇ : M. xxiv. 49ᵇ-51ᵃ : L. xii. 46ᶜ : M. xxiv. 51ᵇ.

E₍ₘ₎ 218.

Who will be the steward, the servant faithful, kind, and wise[1] ? . . . him he shall cut asunder in the midst, and

---

[1] Sc. (L. xii. 42.) Who is the authorized person, faithful, and wise, and good?

The text seems like a compilation from M. and L. (Zahn.)

shall separate him, and apportion his place with the hypo-
crites (M) and unbelievers (L)[1] and there he shall have
weeping of the eyes, and gnashing of the teeth.

✠

§ 131. THE TEN VIRGINS AND THE TALENTS.
Ac—M. xxv. 1-30.

Ea 218.

Five of them were foolish, and five wise.
His talents.   He hid it.   Take from him the talent.

✠

§ 132. LET YOUR LOINS BE GIRDED ABOUT AND YOUR LIGHTS BURNING.
Ac—L. xii. 35-38.

Ea 219.

Let your loins be girded about and your lights burning.

✠

§ 133. JUDGMENT OF ALL THE NATIONS.
Ac—M. xxv. 31-46.

Ea *No ref.*

✠

§ 134. THE PRIESTS AND JUDAS CONSPIRE.
Ac—M. xxvi. 1-5 : L. xxii. 2ᵉ-4ᵃ: M. xxvi. 15ᵃ: Mar. xiv. 11ᵃ:
M. xxvi. 15ᵇ: L. xxii. 6.

Ea *No ref.*

✠

§ 135. CHRIST AS A SERVANT.
Ac—Mar. xiv. 12: J. xiii. 1-20: L. xxii. 27-30.

Ea *No ref.*

---

[1] Notice the wonderful agreement with Arabic.

§ 136. Christ sends two Disciples to prepare the Passover, and announces that one of the Twelve will Betray Him.

A𝒸—L. xxii. 7–10ᵃ : Mar. xiv. 13ᵇ : L. xxii. 10ᵇ, 11ᵃ : M. xxvi. 18ᵇ : L. xxii. 11ᵇ, 12 : Mar. xiv. 15ᶜ, 16 : L. xxii. 14–16 : J. xiii. 21ᵃ : Mar. xiv. 18ᵇ–20 : L. xxii. 21 : Mar. xiv. 21 : J. xiii. 22 : L. xxii. 23 : J. xiii. 23–29 : M. xxvi. 25 : J. xiii. 30–32.

Eₘ 219, 220.

One of you who eateth bread with me, that is he who shall betray me. (Mar.) And behold the hand of my betrayer is stretched out with me on the table. (L.) And the Son of Man goeth as it is written of him. (M. Mar.) It were better for him if he had not been born.

✠

§ 137. Institution of the Eucharist.
A𝒸—Mar. xiv. 22ᵃ: M. xxvi. 26ᵇ: Mar. xiv. 23ᵃ: M. xxvi. 27ᵇ: Mar. xiv. 23ᵇ, 24ᵃ: M. xxvi. 28, 29 : L. xxii. 19ᵇ.

Eₘ 221, 222.

The Lord blessed and brake. Hereafter I will not drink of this fruit of the vine, until the Kingdom of my Father.

✠

§ 138. The Lord prays for Peter: gives His Disciples a New Commandment: and announces that they shall all desert Him that night. Peter's self-confidence.
A𝒸—L. xxii. 31, 32 : J. xiii. 33–36 : M. xxvi. 31–33 : L. xxii. 33ᵇ : J. xiii. 37ᵇ, 38ᵃ : Mar. xiv. 30ᵇ : L. xxii. 34ᵇ : Mar. xiv. 31.

Eₘ 222.

Behold Satan has received permission to sift you as wheat, and I have prayed my Father for thee, that thy faith fail not.

✠

§ 139. He Comforts His Disciples.
A𝒸—J. xiv. 1–31ᵃ.

Eₘ 222, 223.

Show us the Father and it sufficeth us. Have ye not known me ? He who believeth in me, the works which I do shall

he also do. ·He has found nothing of his own[1] in me.
And I have overcome the world. (J. xvi. 33.)

✠

§ 140. Command to provide Swords.

A.—L. xxii. 35-38.

E. 223. 224.

He who hath no sword of his own, let him buy himself a
sword. Two are enough.[2]

✠

§ 141. Jesus' Last Words to His Disciples.

A.—J. xiv. 31[b] : L. xxii. 39 : J. xv., xvi.

E. 224-227.

This is my commandment, Love one another, as I have
loved you. Greater love than this no one can have, than
if any one lay down his life for his friends. Behold I send
you the Paraclete. Another Paraclete I send you. (J. xiv.
16.) It is good for you that I go away, for if I go not away
the Paraclete will not come to you, and all the truth will not
become known to you. But of judgment because the
prince of this world has been condemned.

✠

§ 142. The Prayer of Jesus.

A.—J. xvii.

E. 227, 228.

The hour has come and is now ; glorify thy Son, and thy
Son shall glorify thee. Give me glory from thyself, out of
that which thou gavest me before the world was made
(*v.l.* which I had with thee before the world was.)

---

[1] Zahn cites, as illustrations of this reading, Epiph. Haer. 66, 67 :
Petav., p. 680.
[2] Sc. Our Lord, lo, we have here two swords. He saith to them,
They are enough.

§ 143. In Gethsemane.

Ac—J. xviii. 1, 2 : L. xxii. 40ᵃ : M. xxvi. 36ᵇ : L. xxii. 40ᵇ : M.
xxvi. 37–8 : L. xxii. 41 : Mar. xiv. 35ᵇ, 36ᵃ : L. xxii. 42:
M. xxvi. 40 : Mar. xiv. 37ᵇ : M. xxvi. 40ᵇ, 41ᵃ : Mar. xiv. 38ᵇ:
M. xxvi. 42 : Mar. xiv. 40 ; M. xxvi. 44 : L. xxii. 43–45ᵃ, 46ᵃ :
M. xxvi. 45ᵇ : Mar. xiv. 41ᵇ, 42ᵃ.

Eₘ 228–235.

My soul is sorrowful. If it be possible let this cup pass
from me. (M.) Father let this cup pass from me. (L.)
Not as my will, but as thine. (M.) Not my will be done,
but thine. (L.) And he said to his disciples, Watch and
pray that ye enter not into temptation : this spirit is prompt
and ready, but this flesh is weak. (M. Mar.) And his
sweat became as drops of blood. (L.) Sleep, and take your
rest.

✠

§ 144. Judas and his Party come to seize Jesus. Peter and Malchus. The Disciples flee.

Ac—M. xxvi. 46ᵇ–48 : Mar. xiv. 44ᵇ : J. xviii. 4 : M. xxvi. 49. 50 :
L. xxii. 48ᵇ : M. xxvi. 50ᵃ : L. xxii. 52ᵃ : J. xviii. 4ᵇ–9 :
M. xxvi. 50ᵇ : L. xxii. 49 : J. xviii. 10, 11 : M. xxvi. 52ᵇ–54 :
L. xxii. 51ᵇ : M. xxvi. 55 : L. xxii. 53ᵇ : M. xxvi. 56 :
J. xviii. 12.

Eₘ 235–237.

Judas, comest thou to betray the Son of Man with a
kiss ? (L.) Well, friend, for what hast thou come ? (M.)
Whom seek ye ? They say to him, Jesus of Nazareth.
Jesus said to them, I am he. While yet Judas was standing
with them, they went backwards and fell prostrate on the
ground.
Turn thy sword again into its place. They bound him
and led him away.

✠

§ 145. The Young Man. Peter's First Denial.

Ac—Mar. xiv. 51, 52 : J. xviii. 13–17 : L. xxii. 57 : Mar. xiv. 68ᵇ :
J. xviii. 18ᵃ : L. xxii. 55ᵃ : J. xviii. 18ᵇ : M. xxvi. 58ᵇ.

Eₘ *No ref.*

§ 146. THE HIGH PRIEST QUESTIONS JESUS. PETER'S SECOND AND THIRD DENIALS.

A.—J. xviii. 19-25 : Mar. xiv. 69 : M. xxvi. 71ᵇ, 73ᵃ, 72 : L. xxii. 58ᵃ : J. xviii. 26ᵃ : L. xxii. 59ᵇ : M. xxvi. 73ᵇ : J. xviii. 26ᵇ : Mar. xiv. 71 : L. xxii. 60ᵇ, 61ᵃ : Mar. xiv. 30 : L. xxii. 62.

E. 237.

Henceforth ye shall see the Son of Man, that he comes in bright clouds, with the angels of the heavens.   Then the High Priest put his hand to the borders of his garment, and rent his robe.[1]

✠

§ 147. FALSE WITNESSES.

A.—L. xxii. 66 : M. xxvii. 1ᵇ & xxvi. 59ᵇ, 60ᵃ : Mar. xiv. 59 : M. xxvi. 60ᵇ : Mar. xiv. 57ᵇ-59 : M. xxvi. 63ᵃ : Mar. xiv. 60ᵃ : M. xxvi. 62ᵇ : Mar. xiv 61ᵃ.

E. *No ref.*

✠

§ 148. CONDEMNED FOR BLASPHEMY.

A.—L. xxii. 66ᵇ-68 : M. xxvi. 63ᵇ, 64ᵃ : L. xxii. 70 : M. xxvi. 64ᵇ : Mar. xiv. 63ᵃ : M. xxvi. 65ᵇ : L. xxii. 71 : Mar. xiv. 64ᵇ : M. xxvi. 66ᵇ : Mar. xiv. 65ᵃ : L. xxii. 63ᵇ : Mar. xiv. 65ᵇ : M. xxvi. 68 : L. xxii. 65.

E. *No ref.*

✠

§ 149. BROUGHT BEFORE PILATE.

A.—J. xviii. 28ᵃ : Mar. xv. 1ᵇ : J. xviii. 28ᵇ : M. xxvii. 11ᵃ : J. xviii. 29, 30 : L. xxiii. 2ᵇ : J. xviii. 31-38ᵃ.

E. 238.

And they took him and led him to the gate,[2] and gave him into the hands of Pilate ; and they themselves entered not into the inner parts, into the judgment hall, lest they should be defiled ; that they might first eat the lamb in holiness. (He forbids to give tribute to Cæsar.)

✠

§ 150. BEFORE HEROD. PILATE'S WIFE.

A.—L. xxiii. 4-16, 18ᵃ : Mar. xv. 3 : M. xxvii. 12-14, 19.

E. *No ref.*

---

[1] The words which follow in E are curious : "because he was influenced by the power of new wine."

[2] "Porta," which Moesinger paraphrases by "tribunal."

§ 151. BARABBAS.

A꜀—M. xxvii. 15–17ᵃ : J. xviii. 39, 40 : L. xxiii. 19 : Mar. xv. 8, 9ᵃ :
M. xxvii. 17ᵇ, 18, 20–22 : Mar. xv. 13 : L. xxiii. 20–3 : Mar. xv.
15ᵃ : L. xxiii. 25ᵃ.

Eₘ *No ref.*

✠

§ 152. SCOURGING, SHAME AND SPITTING.

A꜀— M. xxvii. 26ᵇ–28 : J. xix. 2 : M. xxvii. 29ᵇ, 30 : J. xix. 3ᶜ.

Eₘ 239.

(A purple robe.) A crown of thorns. And they spit
upon his face. They gave the reed into his hand.

✠

§ 153. ECCE HOMO! PILATE YIELDS.

A꜀—J. xix. 4–15 : M. xxvii. 24, 25 : J. xix. 16ᵃ.

Eₘ 238, 239.

Away with this man from us, away from us. Shall I
crucify your king ?

✠

§ 154. SUICIDE OF JUDAS.

A꜀—M. xxvii. 3–10.

Eₘ 239–241.

When Judas saw that the Lord was condemned, driven
by grief he went away, and brought back the thirty silver
pieces to the priests, and said, I have sinned, in that I have
betrayed innocent blood. They say to him, We care not :
thou knowest. . . . And he cast the silver into the temple,
and departed, and hanged himself, and died. It is not
lawful to take this silver into the treasury. With it they
bought a burying place.

✠

§ 155. THE CRUCIFIXION.

A꜀—J. xix. 16ᵇ : Mar. xv. 20ᶜ : J. xix. 17ᵃ : M. xxvii. 31ᵇ, 32ᵃ :
Mar. xv. 21ᵇ : M. xxvii. 32ᵇ : L. xxiii. 26ᵇ–33ᵃ : J. xix. 17ᶜ :
L. xxiii. 33ᵇ : Mar. xv. 28, 23ᵃ : M. xxvii. 34ᵇ : Mar. xv. 23ᶜ :
J. xix. 23, 24 : M. xxvii. 36 : J. xix. 19–22 : L. xxiii. 35ᵃ :
M. xxvii. 39, 40ᵃ : Mar. xv. 29ᵇ : M. xxvii. 40ᵇ, 41, 42 :
L. xxiii. 35ᵇ : M. xxvii. 42ᵇ, 43 : L. xxiii. 36, 37.

Eₘ 241–245.

And when he had taken up the wood of his cross, and

had fainted, they found and laid hold of a certain man of Cyrene, and upon him they laid the wood of the cross.

If they do this thing in a green tree. That it might be fulfilled which was spoken, He was reckoned with the transgressors. This is the Christ, the King of the Jews. And they gave him to drink vinegar and poison. He saved others, himself he cannot save.

✠

§ 156. THE WORDS FROM THE CROSS.

A_c—M. xxvii. 44 : L. xxiii. 39-43 : J. xix. 25-27 : M. xxvii. 45ᵃ : L. xxiii. 44ᶜ, 45ᵃ : Mar. xv. 34 : M. xxvii. 47 : J. xix. 28, 29ᵃ : M. xxvii. 48ᵃ : Mar. xv. 36ᵇ : J. xix. 30ᵃ : M. xxvii. 49 : L. xxiii. 34ᵃ, 46ᵃ : J. xix. 30ᵇ.

E_m 242-256.

Art not thou the Christ[1] ? Save thyself and us with thee. (E_m 242).

Lord, remember me in thy kingdom. To-day shalt thou be with me in the garden of delight[2]. (E_m 243-4).

My God, my God, why hast thou forsaken me? Let us see if Elias comes that he may cause him to come down. (E_m 247).

Into thy hands I commend my spirit. (E_m 254).

(Forgive them for they know not what they do. E_m 256).

✠

§ 157. OCCURRENCES AT CHRIST'S DEATH.

A_c—M. xxvii. 51-54ᵃ : L. xxiii. 47ᵇ : M. xxvii. 54ᵇ : L. xxiii. 48.

E_m 245.

Woe was, woe was to us[3], the Son of God was this !

✠

§ 158. CHRIST'S SIDE PIERCED.

A.— J. xix. 31-37.

E_m 259.

And one of the soldiers struck him with a spear.

---

[1] Sc. Art not thou the Messia? Save thyself and save us, also us.
[2] Sc. In the Eden's garden.
[3] Sc. Woe to us, what is this! Woe to us from our sins. See Westcott and Hort, N. T. notes, p. 71. a.

§ 159. THE WOMEN STANDING AFAR OFF.

A_c—L. xxiii. 49ª : Mar. xv. 41ᵇ : M. xxvii. 56ª : Mar. xv. 40ᵇ :
M. xxvii. 56ᶜ : Mar. xv. 40ᵈ, 41 : L. xᴧiii. 49ᶜ.

Eₘ 258.

The relations of Jesus were standing afar off.

✠

§ 160. JOSEPH OF ARIMATHEA.

A_c—Mar. xv. 42 : L. xxiii. 50 : J. xix. 38ᵇ : L. xxiii. 51 : Mar. xv.
43ᵇ–45ª : M. xxvii. 58ᵇ : Mar. xv. 46ª : J. xix. 38ᵇ–42 :
M. xxvii. 60ᵇ.

Eₘ 206.

Joseph.

✠

§ 161. THE WOMEN PREPARE SPICES. THE JEWS SEAL THE TOMB.

A_c—Mar. xv. 47ª : L. xxiii. 55ᵇ, 56ª : Mar. xvi. 1ᵇ : L. xxiii. 56ᵇ :
M. xxvii. 62ᵇ–66.

Eₘ 266.

They sealed his tomb.

✠

§ 162. THE WOMEN COME EARLY TO THE TOMB. THE RESURRECTION. THE TWO ANGELS.

A_c—M. xxviii. 1ª : L. xxiv. 1ª : M. xxviii. 1ᵇ : L. xxiv. 1ᵇ : Mar.
xvi. 3, 4ᵇ : M. xxviii. 2ª : L. xxiv. 2 : M. xxviii. 2ᶜ–4 : L.
xxiv. 3 : Mar. xvi. 5ᵇ : M. xxviii. 5, 6 : L. xxiv. 4–7 : M.
xxviii. 7ª : Mar. xvi. 7ᵇ : M. xxviii. 7ᶜ : L. xxiv. 8 : M. xxviii.
8ª : Mar. xvi. 8ᵇ.

Eₘ *No ref.*

✠

§ 163. MARY OF MAGDALA.

A_c—J. xx. 2–17 : Mar. xvi. 9.

Eₘ 268–271.

If thou hast taken him away . . . Touch me not, for I
have not yet ascended to my Father : go tell my brethren,
I ascend to my Father, and your Father, and to my God
and your God.

§ 164. The Guardsmen bribed to tell a Falsehood.
A.—M. xxviii. 11ᵇ-15.
E. 267, 268.

His disciples stole him away while we slept.

✠

§ 165. Jesus appears to the Women.
Aᶜ—J. xx. 18: M. xxviii. 8ᵇ-10 : L. xxiv. 9 : Mar. xvi. 10ᵇ: L. xxiv. 10 : Mar. xvi. 11 : L. xxiv. 11ᵃ.
E. *No ref.*

✠

§ 166. The Walk to Emmaus.
Aᶜ—Mar. xvi. 12ᵃ: L. xxiv. 13ᵇ-35 : Mar. xvi. 13ᵇ.
E. *No ref.*

✠

§ 167. Jesus appears in the Upper Room.
Aᶜ—L. xxiv. 36ᵃ: J. xx. 19 : L. xxiv. 36ᵇ-49ᵃ: J. xx. 20ᵇ-23.
E. *No ref.*

✠

§ 168. Thomas.
Aᶜ—J. xx. 24-31.
E. *No ref.*

✠

§ 169. At the Sea of Tiberias.
Aᶜ—J. xxi. 1-24.
E. 271-273.

Follow me.   He turned round and looked and saw that disciple, and says to him, And this man, Lord, what?   He said to him (If I will) what is this to thee?

§ 170.· Christ's Commission to His Apostles and His Ascension.

A*c*—M. xxviii. 16, 17 : Mar. xvi. 14 : M. xxviii. 18 : J. xx. 21ᵇ: Mar. xvi. 15ʰ: M. xxviii. 19, 20 : Mar. xvi. 16–18 : L. xxiv. 49ᵇ: Mar. xvi. 19ᵃ: L. xxiv. 50, 51 : Mar. xvi. 19ᶜ: L. xxiv. 52, 53 : Mar. xvi. 20 : J. xxi. 25.

Eₘ 274.

But ye shall remain in Jerusalem until ye shall receive the promise of my Father.

APPENDIX A.

The old theory that the Diatessaron was composed in
Greek (see p. x.) has still an exponent in Professor Harnack.
He says in his article TATIAN in the *Encyclopædia Britan-
nica*, 1888. "It (*i.e.* the Diatessaron) was written by Tatian
in Greek, not in Syriac as Zahn has tried to make out ; this
is shown—(1) by the title, it being known even among the
Syrians as *Diatessaron ;* (2) by a few Greek fragments which
still survive ; (3) by the Latin redaction which it received in
the 6th century ; (4) by its rejection in the Muratorian frag-
ment—for that the word ' m-tia-i,' carelessly corrected by
the transcriber, stood originally ' tatiani,' may be regarded
as certain."

A very few words will suffice in answer to (2) (3) and (4).
With regard to (2), even if Greek fragments survived they
would not prove a Greek original. But it may well be
doubted whether any such fragments survive at all. Ottmar
Nachtigall or Luscinius (see Appendix C) professes to have
translated his Latin Epitome from some Greek fragments,
but if so they could not have been anything but an *Epitome*
founded on the Diatessaron, as will be evident to anyone
who reads Ottmar's publication. It is quite clear that the
work is in no sense a *translation* of the Diatessaron, or of
fragments of it, but that it bears much the same relationship
to it which the chapter headings of our A. V. bear to the
chapters themselves.

By argument (3) Harnack implies that the Latin Version
found in the 6th century could have come only from a Greek
original. This argument has been refuted by anticipation on
p. xxv. See especially the authorities cited in the note.

No. (4) cannot even by courtesy be called an " argument."
It is a mere guess. Dr. Salmon (Article *Muratorian Frag-
ment*, Smith's D. C. B.) says that in this case all that Harnack
Zeitscht. f. Luth. Theol. 1874, p. 276) " succeeds in proving
(if he does succeed) is that it is not beyond the bounds of
possibility that copyists might have perverted ' Tatiani '
into ' Metiadi.' " See also Zahn pp. 9 foll.

There remains then the solitary argument (1) that Tatian

must have compiled his work in Greek, because he gave it a Greek name. But this by no means follows. King Charles did not write his *Eikon Basilike* in Greek, nor Dr. Pusey his *Eirenikon*. Nor could we imagine anyone contending that a collection of opinions on some doctrinal point must have been written in Greek, because its compiler called it a *Symposium*. It is manifest that there are at least two suppositions other than that of a Greek original by which the use of the name *Diatessaron* may be explained. Either Tatian, a man fluent in both Greek and Syriac, may have given to his novel composition the novel name *Diatessaron*, borrowing this from the Greek, introducing it into ecclesiastical terminology, and transliterating it into Syriac, according to the analogy of many other technical ecclesiastical words, as *perikope, katechismos, chronikon, ekklesiastike, diatheke, kephalaion, euangelion,* and especially *tetraeuangelion.*[1]   Or else, as Bäthgen[2] thinks, the word *Diatessaron* may have been already adopted into Syriac, and familiar to the Syrians, as a technical musical,[3] or, it may be added, medical[4] term, and Tatian may have merely employed it in a new and derived signification.

"Anyhow," even according to the Greek hypothesis, "why did not the translator translate the title? I suppose Harnack would say, because he could get no Syriac word to express the same meaning. If so, I don't suppose Tatian could either, which would quite account for his giving a Greek title to his Syriac work."[5]

---

[1] Zahn, p. 104, note 2.
[2] *Der Griechische Text des Cur. Syr. Einleit*, p. 89.
[3] cf. Dr. Mahaffy's note in Salmon Introd. p. 82.
[4] cf. Dr. Quarry's note *ibid.*
[5] Comment by the Rev. H. Jackson Lawlor, B.D.

APPENDIX B.

XXVII.   de relinquendo munus ad altare
XXVIII.   de adulterio concupiscentiae
XXVIIII.   de repudio
XXX.   de iuramento
XXXI.   de oculum pro oculo
XXXII.   de diligendo proximum
XXXIII.   de occulta elemosyna
XXXIIII.   de secreta oratione
XXXV.   de occulto ieiunio
XXXVI.   de non thesaurizando super terram
XXXVII.   quia nemo potest duobus dominis seruire
XXXVIII.   non debere solliciti esse de esca uel de indu-
            mento
XXXVIIII.   non debere quemquam iudicare uel condem-
            nare
XL.   parabola de amico uel de tribus panibus peten-
            dum quaerendum pulsandum
XLI.   de cauendo a falsis prophetis
XLII.   non hi intrabunt in regno caelorum qui tantum
            dicunt domine domine
XLIII.   conparatio in his omnibus.   de sapiente et insi-
            piente aedificatoribus
XLIIII.   ubi ihesus mittit XII discipulos suos docere et
            curare omnes infirmitates
XLV.   ubi ihesus in chanan galileae aqua uinum fecit.
XLVI.   ubi ihesus mundat leprosum
XLVII.   ubi ihesus puerum centurionis paralyticum
            curauit
XLVIII.   ubi socrum petri a febribus sanauit ihesus
XLVIIII.   ubi ihesus in ciuitatem naim mortuum resusci-
            tauit
L.   ubi omnes infirmitates curat. ut adinplerentur
            scribturae prophetarum
LI.   ubi uolenti eum sequi dixit. uulpes foueas.
            habent
LII.   ubi nauigans increpauit tempestati et cessauit
LIII.   Ubi curauit trans fretum daemoniacum qui in.
            monumentis manebant
LIIII.   Ubi curauit paralyticum quem deposuerunt per
            tectum
LV.   Ubi filium subreguli absentem curauit
LVI.   Ubi leui publicanus conuiuium ei fecit.   Et
            dicentes scribae et pharisaei discipulis. quare
            cum publicanis et peccatoribus manducat
            magister uester

LXXVIIII.   Ubi ihesus in deserto de quinque panibus v
milia hominum saturauit

LXXX.   Ubi ihesus supra mare pedibus ambulauit. et
petrum mergentem liberat

LXXXI.   Ubi transfretantes uenerunt in terram gennesar.
et turbae secutae sunt trans mare de manna in
deserto

LXXXII.   de murmuratione iudaeorum. eo quod ait ihesus
ego sum panis uiuus

LXXXIII.   Ubi quidam pharisaeus rogauit ihesum ad
prandium et cogitabat quare non fuerit bap-
tizatus

LXXXIIII.   de apostolis quare non lotis manibus manduca-
runt

LXXXV.   de muliere syrophonissa quae pro filia sua
petebat

LXXXVI.   Ubi ihesus super puteum iacob. mulieri samari-
tanae locutus est

LXXXVII.   Ubi ihesus surdum et mutum curauit

LXXXVIII.   Ubi hierosolymis infirmum curauit. qui xxxviii
annis iacuit infirmitate et multa cum iudaeis
eius occasione disputavit

LXXXVIIII.   Ubi ihesus de vii panes. et paucos pisces IIII
hominum saturauit. et praecepit apostolis
cauere a fermento pharisaeorum

XC.   Ubi ihesus interrogat apostolos. quem me
dicunt homines esse et quae secuntur et dicit
petro scandalum mihi es

XCI.   Ubi ihesus dicit et quidam astantibus non gustare mortem et in monte transfiguratur

XCII.   Ubi pharisaei dicunt ad ihesum. discede hinc
quia herodes uult te occidere et curauit luna-
ticum

XCIII.   Ubi ihesus de passione sua. discipulis patefecit.
et capharnaum pro se. et petro didragma
exactoribus reddit

XCIIII.   Ubi ihesus interrogatus a discipulis suis. quis
maior erit in regno caelorum instruit eos his
exemplis ut humilient se sicut paruulus

XCV.   Non debere prohiberi eos qui faciunt signa in
nomine ihesu

XCVI.   Non debere contemnere unum de pusillis adiungens similitudinem de oue perdita et de
dragma

XCVII.   de filio qui substantiam patris deuorauit

xcviii.   de remittendo fratribus ex corde

xcviiii.   Similitudo de rege qui posuit rationem cum seruis suis

c.   Ubi ihesus interrogatur a pharisaeis si liceat uxorem dimittere quacumque ex causa

ci.   Ubi ihesus imposuit manum infantibus et pharisaei murmurant de ihesu quod sic recipit peccatores

cii.   Ubi ihesus sanat in synagoga mulierem aridam et curbatam

ciii.   Ubi ihesus ascendit hierosolyma in die festo scenopegiae

ciiii.   Ubi ihesus instruit eos qui annuntiauerunt ei de galilaeis. quos interfecit pilatus. adiungens similitudinem arboris fici in uinea.

cv.   Non debere prohiberi eos qui faciunt signa in nomine ihesu

cvi.   Non debere contemnere unum de pusillis. adiungens similitudinem de oue perdita et de dragma

cvii.   de diuite et lazaro

cviii.   de uilico infidele

cviiii.   de patre familias qui exiit primo mane conducere mercennarios in uineam suam

cx.   Ubi in domo pharisaei sanat ihesus hydropicum et instruit eos qui primos accubitus in conuiuiis eligebant

cxi.   Ubi ihesus x leprosos mundauit

cxii.   Ubi ihesus de passione sua discipulis suis iterum indicauit et mater filiorum zebedaei rogat pro filiis suis

cxiii.   Ubi ihesus responsum dat dicenti sibi. domine pauci sunt qui salui fiant

cxiiii.   de zaccheo publicano

cxv.   Ubi ihesus iterum duos caecos curauit

cxvi.   Ubi ihesus asinum sedens hierosolyma ingreditur

cxvii.   Ubi ihesus eicit de templo ementes et uendentes et dat responsum pharisaeis

cxviii.   Ubi ihesus praetulit ceteris uiduam propter duo aera minuta. adiungens parabulam de pharisaeo et publicano contra eos qui se extollunt

cxviiii.   de nicodemo qui uenit ad ihesum nocte

cxx.   de muliere a iudæis in adulterio deprehensa

cxxi.   Ubi ihesus maledixit ficulneam et aruit

CXXII. Ubi ihesus dicit parabolam ad discipulos propter orandi instantiam. de iudice duro et uidua

CXXIII. Ubi ihesus interrogatura principibus sacerdotum. in qua potestate haec facis. adiungens parabulam de duobis filiis in uineam missis

CXXIIII. parabulam de patre familias. qui uineam suam locauit agricolis

CXXV. Simile est regnum caelorum homini regi qui fecit nuptias filio suo

CXXVI. Ubi pharisaei mittunt ad ihesum dolo interrogantes. si licet tributum reddere caesari

CXXVII. de sadducaeis qui dicunt non esse resurrectionem et interrogant de VII fratribus. qui unam uxorem habuerunt

CXXVIII. Ubi scriba interrogat ihesum quod mandatum maximum est in lege

CXXVIIII. Ubi docente ihesu in templo miserunt pharisaei eum comprehendere

CXXX. Ubi ihesus interrogat pharisaeos. cuius filius est christus

CXXXI. Ubi ihesus docet. ego sum lux mundi

CXXXII. Ubi ihesus faciens lutum de sputo ponens super oculos caeci nati curauit eum

CXXXIII. Ubi ihesus agnitus est eidem caeco et contendit multa cum iudaeis

CXXXIIII. Ubi interrogatur ihesus a iudaeis si tu es christus dic nobis manifeste

CXXXV. Ubi ihesus resuscitat lazarum a mortuis et principes consilium faciunt ut interficerent ihesum

CXXXVI. Ubi non receptus in ciuitate samaritana. iohannes et iacobus dicunt ad ihesum si uis dicimus ut ignis discendat de caelo

CXXXVII. Ubi ihesus uenit in bethaniam et multi iudaeorum euntes propter lazarum crediderunt in eum

CXXXVIII. Ubi maria fudit alabastrum ungenti in capite ihesu. et increpat pharisaeo

CXXXVIIII. Ubi hierosolymis graeci uidere uolunt ihesum

CXL. Ubi pharisaei interrogant ihesum. quando uenit regnum dei

CXLI. Ubi ihesus loquitur ad turbas et discipulos de scribis et pharisaeis

CXLII. Ubi ihesus lamentat super hierusalem

CXLIII.   Ubi multi ex principibus crediderunt in eum et non confitebantur ne de synagoga eicerentur

CXLIIII.   Ubi ostendunt discipuli ihesu structuram templi

CXLV.   Ubi sedente ihesu. in montem oliueti interro-gant eum discipuli. quod signum erit aduen-tus tui uel eorum quae dixisti. et praedicat eis. de euersione hierusalem et signis et prodigiis

CXLVI.   de parabola ficulneae

CXLVII.   Ubi ihesus diem iudicii aduersus tempora noe et loth adsimilauit. et de fidele et prudente dispensatore

CXLVIII.   de decem uirginibus

CXLVIIII.   de eo qui peregre proficiscens talenta seruis suis distribuit

CL.   Ut lumbi semper praecincti sint et lucernae ardentes

CLI.   de eo qui peregre accipere sibi regnum proficis-cens x mnas seruis suis dedit

CLII.   Cum uenerit filius hominis in sede maiestatis suae

CLIII.   Ubi iterum consilium faciunt principes et uadit iudas ad eos

CLIIII.   Ubi ihesus lauat pedes discipulorum

CLV.   Ubi ihesus mittet discipulos praeparare sibi pascha et dicit eis quod unus ex uobis tradit me

CLVI.   Ubi ihesus tradet de sacramento corporis et sanguinis sui

CLVII.   Ubi ihesus dicit ad petrum. expetiuit satanas ut uos uentilet. et omnes hodie in me scan-dalizamini

CLVIII.   Ubi ihesus hortatur discipulos suos ut non pauefiat cor uestrum

CLVIIII.   Ubi ihesus dicit discipulis suis qui quod habet baiulet

CLX.   Ubi ihesus dicit. ego sum uitis et uos palmites

CLXI.   Ubi ihesus uenit in gesemani et orat ut trans-ferat calicem istum

CLXII.   Ubi iudas uenit cum turbis comprehendere ihesum

CLXIII.   Ubi adulescens quidam indutus sindone seque-batur ihesum

CLXIIII.   Ubi interrogat princeps sacerdotum ihesum de discipulis et de doctrina eius.

CLXV.   Ubi falsi testes aduersus ihesum quaerebantur

CLXVI.   Ubi principes sacerdotum adiurat ihesum. si tu es christus dic nobis

CLXVII.   Ubi traditur pilato ihesus et paenitetur iudas

CLXVIII.   Ubi pilatus audit inter iudaeos et dominum et mittit eum ad herodem

CLXVIIII.   Ubi uxor pilati misit ad eum dicens nihil tibi sit et iusto illi

CLXX.   Ubi pilatus dimisit barabban. et tradidit chr-is tum ad crucifigendum

CLXXI.   Ubi duo latrones cum christo crucifigi ducuntur. et ubi ihesus de cruce de matre sua dixit ad discipulum quem diligebat. ecce mater tua

CLXXII.   Ubi ioseph petit corpus ihesu a pilato et sepelit una cum nicodemo

CLXXIII.   Ubi iudaei signant monumentum

CLXXIIII.   Ubi prima die sabbati suscitatur ihesus a mortuis

CLXXV.   Ubi custodes monumenti annuntiauerunt sacerdotibus. de resurrectione christi

CLXXVI.   Ubi ihesus apparuit mulieribus post resurrectionem

CLXXVII.   Ubi ihesus duobus euntibus in castellum apparuit

CLXXVIII.   Ubi ihesus apparuit discipulis suis

·CLXXVIIII.   Ubi ihesus iterum apparuit thomæ

CLXXX.   Ubi iterum apparuit ihesus discipulis super mare tiberiadis

CLXXXI.   Ubi ihesus ter dicit petro diligis me

CLXXXII.   Ubi discipuli euntes in galilaeam. uiderunt et adorauerunt dominum et assumptus est in cælis coram eis

APPENDIX C.

THE EPITOME CONSTRUCTED FROM SOME GREEK FRAGMENTS
BY LUSCINIUS.

OTTMAR NACHTIGALL, the Humanist, who styled himself Luscinius, was born at Strasbourg, A.D. 1487. After studying at Paris, Louvain, Padua, and Vienna, and travelling through many countries of Europe and Asia, he settled at Augsburg, where he gave lessons in Greek. He afterwards moved to Fribourg. He was a great opponent of the Reformation, the leaders of which, Luther and von Hütten, were the object of his bitter satires. The title of the work which he published at Augsburg, 4to, A.D. 1523, is *Evangelicae historiae ex quatuor Evangelistis perpetuo tenore continuata narratio, ex Ammonii Alexandrini fragmentis quibusdam, e Graeco per Ottomarum Luscinium versa : qua et tedio sacre (sic) lectionis studiosorum succurrit, et ordine pulcherrimo mire juvat memoria.*

In his Preface Luscinius refers to the corrupt morals and mock philosophies of his time, and prescribes the law of the Lord as the only thing which will do people real lasting good. He, however, excuses himself from translating the four Gospels from the Greek on the ground that he had little leisure, and considers it more profitable that he should weave together one out of the four, and in consecutive order. This will spare the reader trouble, and will assist his memory : for in the Gospel narratives many things are put out of their proper order. To the possible objection that he is thus seeking to supersede the Canonical Gospels, he replies that he is only following the example of such men as Juvencus, Augustine, Eusebius, and more especially Ammonius of Alexandria "*in cujus fragmenta jampridie incidimus, modo fallax non sit titulus. Quem quidem e Graeco vertimus per otium, etc.*"

From the whole tone of this Preface, and from the character of the work itself, it is likely that Luscinius handled his Greek fragments with great freedom, not so much translating them into Latin, as constructing a Latin Epitome on the lines which they suggested. That these Greek fragments had been in some way derived from

Tatian's Diatessaron is evident from the numerous coincidences in erroneous order which anyone can see between
the Diatessaron and the Luscinian Epitome, as represented
by the following table of contents which I have made. Note
the *order* in which the Diatessaron, the Codex Fuldensis,
and the Epitome of Luscinius agree in presenting the
following :—

- (A.)   Tne first words of S. John's Gospel.
- (B.)   The Episode about Martha and Mary.
- (C.)   The Mission of the Seventy.
- (D.)   The rejection at Nazareth.
- (E.)   The discourse on the Bread of Life.
- (F.)   The Syrophenician or Canaanite woman.
- (G.)   The infirm man at Bethesda.
- (H.)   The parables in S. Luke xv.
- (I.)   The murdered Galileans.
- (J.)   The *Skenopegia*.
- (K.)   The visit of Nicodemus.
- (L.)   The mission of the officers to sieze Jesus.

It is remarkable that a German translation of the Epitome
in which Tatian's name occurs was published at Augsburg,
8vo, A.D. 1524.[1] So that the doubt about the Ammonian
authorship, which Luscinius had expressed the year before,
seems to have given place to a sure conviction that the
work was ultimately traceable to Tatian.

Zahn (pp. 313-328), gives a tolerably full discussion of
the origin of this Epitome : he does not think (p. 327) that
it was derived from the Harmony found by Victor.

---

[1] Several other Edd. of the Epitome were published, as Basle, 1555 :
Cologne, 1618.

TABLE OF CONTENTS

OF THE

EPITOME OF LUSCINIUS.[1]

In the beginning was the Word.
Joseph's doubts satisfied by the angel.
The visit of Gabriel to Mary.
Joseph warned in a dream.
The taxing, birth of Christ, angels and shepherds.
The Magi.
The Circumcision.
The star ; gifts of the Magi.
Simeon and Anna.
Herod's murderous attempt.   Return to Nazareth.
Flight in to Egypt.   Innocents.
Jesus at the age of twelve.
John's preaching.   His baptism, holiness, austerity.   His
    confession.
Jesus at the age of thirty ; baptized by John ; voice from
    heaven.
Temptation.
Some of John's disciples follow Jesus.
Marriage at Cana.
First cleansing of the temple.
First miraculous draught.
John's statement, " He must increase," &c.
John's martyrdom.
Jesus goes to Zabulon and Nephthali.

FIRST YEAR OF OUR LORD'S MINISTRY.

The Spirit of the Lord is upon me.
The twelve chosen.
Sermon on Mount.
Mission of the twelve.
The leper.
Centurion's servant (confounded with nobleman's son).
Demoniac in synagogue.
Young man at Nain.

---

[1] In the original Ed., 1523, the Epitome occupies only 45 small 4to
pages of large type.

Many cures. ·Fame through Syria.
Woman, who was a sinner, forgiven.
Foxes have holes, &c.
Tempest stilled.
Demons in swine.
Demoniac (!) let down through roof.
Call of Matthew the publican.
Woman of Samaria.
Nobleman's son at Cana.
Levi's feast.   On fasting.
A sign, Jonah.   Queen of the South.
Return of unclean spirit.
Blessed is the womb.
Christ's mother and brethren seek him.
Jairus' daughter.
Two blind men.
Dumb demoniac.
Pharisees blaspheme.
A good man out of the good treasure, &c.
Martha and Mary.
Mission of the seventy-two.
I beheld Satan, &c.
I thank thee, O Father.
Plucking ears of corn.
Withered hand.
Plot to destroy Jesus.
Night on a mountain in prayer.
Sower.   Tares.   Secret growth.   Mustard.
Leaven.   Hid treasure.   Pearl.   Net.

SECOND YEAR OF OUR LORD'S MINISTRY.

Rejection at Nazareth.
Herod's desire to see Jesus.
Five thousand fed.
Attempt to make Christ a king.
Walks on water.
At Gennesaret cures those who touch hem of garment.
The Bread of Life.
Pharisee's feast.   Traditions.
Hypocrisy of Scribes and Pharisees.
Every plant, &c.
Defilements.
Canaanite woman.
Others seek Jesus at borders of Tyre and Sidon.
Feast of Pentecost.   Infirm man at Bethesda.

Four thousand fed.
At Dalmanutha.   The leaven of the Pharisees.
Peter's confession at Cæsarea Philippi.
Christ foretells his death and resurrection.
Peter rebuked.
On crossbearing.
Transfiguration.
The demoniac boy.
The stater in the fish's mouth.
Dispute as to precedence.   The little child.
Lost sheep, lost silver, prodigal son.
Peter's question as to a sinning brother.
The unmerciful servant.
On divorce.   On celibacy.
Blessing the infants.
The slain Galileans.   The tower in Siloam.   The fig tree.
Cure of the crooked woman.
Herod's threat.
The *skenopegia* at Jerusalem.
Speak to my brother that he divide the inheritance.
The rich fool.
The discourse in S. John viii.
The man blind from his birth.
The rich young ruler.
Peter's question, what shall we have therefore?
Dives and Lazarus.
The unjust steward.
Labourers in vineyard.
At Pharisee's house.   The chief seats.   On inviting the poor.

THIRD YEAR OF OUR LORD'S MINISTRY.

Feast of the *Enkainia*.   Solomon's porch.
Attempt to stone Jesus.
Retreat beyond Jordan.   Lazarus raised.
Plot against Jesus.   Caiaphas.
Jesus goes to Ephraim.
The ten lepers.
The Samaritan village
Jesus predicts his death.
Request of sons of Zebedee.
Zacchæus.
Blind men at Jericho.
At house of Simon the leper.   Christ's head anointed.
Sends two disciples.   Public entry.
The people cry *Osana*.

E

Lament over Jerusalem.
Second cleansing of temple.
Cures blind and lame in temple.
Foretells destruction of temple.
The widow's mites.
Pharisee and publican.
Returns at even to Bethany.
Nicodemus comes to him at night.
Fig tree cursed.
Woman taken in adultery.
Greeks desire to see him   Voice from heaven.
Returns to Bethany at even.
Next morning fig tree withered.
Unjust judge.
By what authority, &c.?
The two sons.
The wicked husbandmen.
Marriage of King's son.
Tribute to Cæsar.
Sadducees' question.
The good Samaritan.
The officers who were sent to apprehend Jesus say, " Never
    man spake like this man."
Discussion as to where the Christ was to be born.
What think ye of the Christ?
Woes on the Scribes and Pharisees.
The splendour of the temple pointed out.
Discourse on Mount of Olives.
On watching.   The faithful steward.
The ten virgins.
The slothful servant.
The sheep and the goats.
Council against Jesus.
Judas agrees to betray him.
Jesus sends two disciples to prepare passover.
Washes disciples' feet.
Indicates that a disciple will betray him.
Institutes the Eucharist.
Peter's self-confidence.   The threefold denial predicted.
A new commandment.
S. John xiv., xv., xvi., xvii.
Gethsemane.   Bloody sweat.   Angel.
Judas and his band.
Peter and Malchus.   .
Disciples flee.

Before Annas.
False witness sought.
Christ proclaims his second advent.
Condemnation.
Peter's denial.
Before Pilate.
Judas relents and dies.
Before Herod.
Barabbas.
Scourging.
Pilate's wife.
Pilate washes his hands.
Between two robbers.
Women bewail.
Father forgive, &c.
To-day shalt thou be with me in Paradise.
Title on the cross.
Christ's raiment.
Mary and John.
My God, my God, why, &c.?
Vinegar given.
Into thy hands, &c.
Darkness, earthquake, graves opened.
The centurion's confession.
Beating their breasts.
Piercing of Jesus' side.
Joseph of Arimathea.
Women watching afar off.
The watch.   The stone.
Resurrection.
The soldiers bribed.
Women with spices.
Angels.
Women relate to disciples.
Peter and John run to tomb.
Jesus appears to Mary of Magdala.
Emmaus.
In upper room.   Jesus breathes on disciples.
Thomas.
At Tiberias.
Mountain in Galilee.
Commission to disciples.
End of S. Mark.

THE Diatessaron exercised influence in Western Christen-
dom through at least two independent channels, the Greek
and the Latin. Of the former we can say nothing more, as
Luscinius is our only authority for its existence. We turn
then to the Latin Harmony which Victor found.

1. The very MS. which was edited under his direction is
still extant in the Codex Fuldensis, so called because preserved at Fulda in Hesse Cassel, where it has been known since
the 14th century, and where tradition says that it has existed
ever since the time of Boniface, the so-called Apostle of Germany, who founded the monastery of Fulda in the middle of
the 8th century. Boniface was a diligent student of Scripture ;
and it is reported on the credit of one who professed to have
witnessed his martyrdom, when an old man, at the hands of
the Frisian Barbarians, that he had a copy of the Gospels
with him then, and held it over his head when he received
the fatal stroke. His body, we know, was brought back all
the way to his beloved Fulda ; and it is supposed that
this book, which had been his companion in life and his
solace in death, was brought back at the same time, and
that it is none other than the codex which we now have.
Internal evidence certainly seems to fall in with the tradition
that the codex belonged to Boniface. The Anglo-Saxon
glosses which are found in it may well have been the work
of him who as Winfried the Englishman must have spoken
Anglo-Saxon as his vernacular. And Ranke[1] has pointed
out several similarities in expression between these glosses
and the undoubted works of Boniface. He notices more
particularly the quotation from 1 Peter in Boniface Ep. 70.
Sobrii estote, et vigilate, et excitamini. These words are not
found in the Cod. Amiatinus, nor in Sabatier's MSS., nor in
the Clementine ed. of the Vulgate, nor in the original hand
of the Cod. Fuldensis, but are in the last named as the
addition of a later hand. It is very likely then that
Boniface may have taken them from thence.

---

[1] From the preface of whose edition of the Cod. Fuld. this portion
of the note has been taken.

If then the Codex really belonged to "the Apostle of Germany," its influence must have been very great during the eighth century.[1]

2. Passing on to the ninth century we find the Harmony, like so many other Latin theological works about the age of Charlemagne, translated into the Eastern Frankish.[2] A large portion[3] of this translation was published at Zurich, by Palthenius, from an Oxford MS., A.D. 1706. A better edition appeared at Ulm, A.D. 1727, in the 2nd vol. of Schilter's *Thesaurus Antiquitatum Teutonicarum* under the title *Tatiani Syri Harmonia Evangelica e Latina Victoris Capuani versione translata in linguam Theotiscam[4] antiquissimam.*

But though the name of Tatian thus appeared on the title page, Schilter and Frickius, the editors, both believed that Victor was mistaken in ascribing his find to the heretic.

3. About the same time as this translation was made, the Monk Ottfried (died A.D. 870), a former pupil of Rhaban Maur at Fulda, wrote his poetical life of Christ in the South Frankish dialect. This work, which is devoid of poetic power, is written in the rhymed stanza, imitated from the Latin, and was doubtless intended to be sung to the accompaniment of the harp. It is very probable that the parentage of Ottfried's work must also be ascribed to the Latin Harmony.[5]

4. But there is a much more worthy descendant of Tatian which had a share in moulding the religious destinies of the West. A book appeared at Munich, A.D. 1830, entitled *Héliand, Poema Saxonicum seculi noni.* This name was given to it by its editor, Schmeller, in recognition of the fact that the poem, which is alliterative, is concerned with a

---

[1] The first printed ed. was that of Maintz, 1525, under the name "*quatuor evangeliorum consonantia.*" Other edd. were Basle, 1555; Cologne, 1618; Lyons, 1677; Migne's ed., 1847; and Ranke's, 1868.

[2] Prof. Sievers in his article *German language.* Encycl. Brit.

[3] All except chap. 76—153, which portion is lost.

[4] Prof. Sievers, Encyc. Brit. clearly proves that this word is only the old form of *Deutsch.* "In Ulphilas' Gothic version of the Bible we have the adv. *thiudisko* (= ἐθνικῶς), Gal. ii. 14, clearly a derivative from *thiuda* = ἔθνος : and German writers of the earlier centuries called their own language *diutisc,* or in a Latinized form *theudiscus, theotiscus* = the popular or vernacular language." Prof. Sievers edited the work, Paderborn, 1872.

[5] The first ed. of this work was published at Basle, 1571. Other editions are Schilter, Ulm, 1727; Graff, Königsberg, 1831; Piper, Paderborn, 1878.

history of the Saviour. And in his Latin preface he says :
"As far as regards the series of Evangelical words and
deeds, we can easily persuade ourselves that the author had
before his eyes that Harmony well known to the ancients
from the beginning of the third century, by Ammonius
(commonly Tatian) of Alexandria, edited in Latin, A.D. 546,
by Victor, Bishop of Capua. This is plain from a comparison of both works since the thread of the narrative seems
identical, a few things only being displaced." Schmeller
goes on to speak of the poem as the greatest monument of
the old Saxon language in existence. He says, "the
whole breathes the spirit of the old Saxon nation and
customs ; and the diction sometimes rises to a very high
pitch of poetic power and beauty. There is no doubt that
the benign and beautiful doctrines of Christianity by soothing
the ears of ignorant heathen would in this way find a ready
access to their hearts."

With regard to the date and authorship, it would seem
from a statement quoted by Schmeller from an old Basle
catalogue, as well as from internal evidence, that the poem
was composed in the reign of Louis the Pious,[1] and was
one of the agents in that policy of conciliation by which he
sought to win over to Christianity the heathen Saxons, who
had for thirty years resisted the efforts of his father Charlemagne. Under the coercionist policy of the last-named
Prince baptism was viewed by the Saxons as merely a badge
of submission to the hated Frankish yoke. And this was
but natural when we remember that he put to death those
of them who refused to submit to this ordinance. Such
policy was of course doomed to failure. The Saxons while
outwardly professing Christianity were still heathens at
heart, and in their primeval forests continued to sing their
old epics in honour of Woden and Thor. And so when
Louis came to the throne he saw clearly that the only way
they could be weaned from these was by the substitution of
Christian epics such as Caedmon had already composed for
the religious instruction of the early English.[2] Thus the
work of Tatian played amid the forests of Saxony a similar
part to that which seven centuries before, in its original

---

[1] It is to be noted that the 9th century was the great era for these
epic poems amongst the nations of Northern Europe, *e.g.*, the Sagas of
Scandinavia.

[2] Alcuin of York, who must have known Caedmon's poetry well, was
the trusted adviser of Louis.

form, it had played upon the banks of the Syrian Euphrates.[1]

5. Another way by which the Latin Diatessaron influenced
the mind of the West was by being made the basis of commentaries. Here again history was found to repeat itself;
for what Ephraem did in the 4th century a writer named
Zacharias of Chrysopolis did about the beginning of the
12th. We know very little of this Zacharias: but his commentary must have had wide currency in his own time, for Alberi-
cus Monachus[2] said (A.D. 1157): *Fecit volumen* ILLUD
EGREGIUM *super quatuor Evangelia quod unum ex quatuor
(Monotessaron) appellatur."* And that it exercised great
influence later is evident from the number of printed editions
which appeared.[3]

From what Zacharias says in his preface we know that he
must have had Victor's preface before him, though he never
mentions it, and plainly rejects the view that the work was
by Tatian. *Matthaei namque dictis reliquorum trium excerpta
arte mira magisque brevitate miranda junguntur. Hoc autem
prenominatum Ammonium fecisse scribit Eusebius Carpiano.*
Here we have the interesting fact that the works of Tatian
and Ammonius were confounded, *because* it appeared that
each had taken St. Matthew as the basis of his harmony
(see Introduction, p. xxx).

Another Commentary on a Gospel Harmony is mentioned
in Montfaucon's Catalogue of MSS. at Bec. This Commentary appears to have been one of the books acquired by
Richard of St. David in the time of Capellanus first Abbot
of Bec. It is founded on the work of Zacharias, and therefore represents the Diatessaron.[4]

---

[1] For the literature of the Hêliand, see art. HELIAND, *Encyc. Brit.*
[2] See Phil. Labbe, Diss. Philol. de Scrip. Eccl. vol. ii., p. 504.
[3] Cologne, 1535 and 1618. Lyons, 1677.
[4] See Fabricius *Script. vet. Graec.* Bk. V. p. 92.

APPENDIX E.

PECULIAR READINGS OF THE EPHRAEM FRAGMENTS IN THEIR RELATION TO
THE ARABIC, THE CURETONIAN, AND THE PESHITTO.

+ signifies that the reading of **E**$_m$ is supported, and — that it is contradicted
by **A**$_o$, Sc, or Pesh.
o is a sign that the authority under which it is placed is here deficient.

Matthew.	**E**$_m$	**A**$_o$	Sc.	Pesh.	
i. 18	*antequam data esset viro* ...	—	—	—	note
,, 25	*sancte habitabat cum ea* ...	—	+	—	
,, ,,	*sumpsit eam* ...	—	—	—	
ii. 11	*aurum et myrrham et thus* ...	+	+	+	
,, 17	*verbum quod dictum est* ...	—	+	—	
iii. 4	*et veste ex pilis cameli* ...	—	—	—	
iv. 3	*in hoc momento* ...	—	—	—	
,, 10	*retro vade Satana* ...	—	+	—	
v. 28	*aspicit et concupiscit adulterat*	—	+	—	
,, 39	*maxillam tuam* ...	—	+	—	
vi. 17	*lava faciem t. et ungue caput tuum* ...	+	+	+	
viii. 5 and Luk. vii. 3	*venit ille cum senioribus populi*	+	—	—	
x. 23	*fugite inde in aliam civitatem; et si ab hac persequentur vos f. denuo in al. civ.* ...	—	o	—	
xi. 25	*pater coelestis* ...	—	—	—	
xii. 22	*demoniacum surdum et mutum et coecum . . . auditum, loquelam et visum* ...	—	partly	—	
xiii. 27	*semen sementis sancti* ...	—	—	—	
xv. 5	*dicitis unicuique* ...	—	partly	partly	
,, 27	*mensae domini sui* ...	—	—	—	
xvi. 13	*quid de me dicunt homines, quod sit filius hominis* ...	—	—	—	
,, 18	*te non vincent* ...	—	—	—	
,, 28	*qui nunc hic mihi assistunt* ...	—	—	—	
xvii. 5	*ipsum audite et vivetis* ...	—	—	—	
,, 17	*O generatio mala perversa et incredula* ...	—	partly	—	
xviii. 20	*ubi unus est, ibi et ego sum: et ubi duo sunt ibi et ego ero*	—	—	—	

Matthew.	E_m	A_c	Sc.	Pesh.	
xviii. 22	*usque septuagies septies septies...*	+	+	+	
xix. 17	*nisi tantum unus pater qui in coelis* ...	—	—	—	
xx. 6	*tota die ad vesperam* ...	—	—	—	
„ 15	*in domo mea* ...	—	—	—	
xxi. 19	*festinans venit* ...	—	—	—	
„ 31	*secundus* ...	—	—	—	
xxii. 23	*et dicunt ei : non est resurrectio mortuorum* ...	+	+	partly	
„ 24	*Moyses patriarcha* ...	—	—	—	
„ 36	*primum et magnum* ...	partly	partly	—-	
xxiv. 20	*orate et petite* ...	—	—	—	
xxvi. 41	*spiritus hic promptus et paratus est sed caro haec infirma*	—	o	—	
„ 65	*manum ad oras vestimenti misit et laceravit stolam suam* ...	—-	o	—	
xxvii. 3	*actus dolore abiit* ...	—	o	—	
„ 5	*et se suspendit et mortuus est* ...	—	o	—	
Mark.					
i. 15	*impleta sunt tempora* ...	—-	o	—	
ii. 14	Evidently James the son of Alphæus ...	—	o	—	note
ix. 25	*immunde surde et mute* ...	—	o	—	
x. 36	*(faciam vobis)* ...	—	o	—	
John.					
i. 1	*a principio* arm A not B ...	—	—	—	
„ 3	*et sine ipso factum est nihil. Quodcunque,* &c. ...	—	+	—	
„ 5	*lucebat* ...	—	+	—	
„ 17	*veritas ejus* (scil. legis) ...	—	—	—	
„ „	*per Jesum Dominum nostrum*	—	—	—	
„ 29	*hic est qui venit tollere* ...	—	partly	—.	
„ 47	*verus scriba Israelita* ...	—	o	—	
ii. 3	*vinum non habent hic* ...	—	o	—	
„ 5	*filius meus* ...	—	o	—-	
iii. 6	*qui natus est* (bis) ...	—	—	—	
„ 13	*qui est in coelo* omitted ...	—	partly	—	see note
iv. 9	*ecce tu Judaeus es* ...	—	+	—	
„ 13	*(mea aqua e coelo descendit)* ..	—	—	—	

John.	E$_m$	A$_c$	Sc.	Pesh.	
iv. 25	*omnia nobis dabit*	—	—	—	
„ 42	*et vidimus opera ejus*	—	—	—	
v. 4	apparently in E's text	contains	omits	contains	
„ 8	*in domum tuam*	—	+	—	
„ 13	*quum multitudinem populi videret*	—	partly	—	
„ 14	*ne alio quodam tibi opus sit*	—	—	—	see note
„ 17	*ideo et ego operor*	—	+	—	
vi. 44	*trahet eum ad ipsum* arm A	—	—	—	
	arm B = *ad me*	—	—	—	
„ 50	*num et morietur* arm A	—	partly	—	
	arm B = *non morietur*				
viii. 44	*filii Satanae*	—	o	—	
ix. 7	*lava faciem tuam*	—	o	—	
xi. 3	*in lecto decumbit*	—	o	—	
„ 11	*L. amicus noster*	+	o	+	D
„ 35	*et lacrymatus est Dominus*	—	o	—	
„ 48	*gentem nostram legem et locum istum*	—	o	—	
xii. 47	*ego non novi eum*	—	o	—	
xiv. 30	*non invenit quidquam suum*	—	o	—	
xvi. 7	*et omnis veritas vobis non innotescet...*	—	o	—	
xviii. 5	*dum adhuc Judas cum eis stabat*	—	o	—	
„ 28	*ad portam*	—	o	—	
„ 28	*ut prius ederent agnum in sanctitate*	—	o	—	
xix. 17	*et exiisset*	+	o	—	
Luke.					
i. 6	*immaculati erant in omni habitatione sua*	—	o	—	
„ 45	*omnium verborum*	—	o	—	
„ 77	*dare scientiam perfectam salutis*	—	o	—	
ii. 11	*(qui Christus Domini jam est)*	—	o	—	Jer. Syr.
„ 14	*(ex libera voluntate)*	—	o	—	
„ „	*(spes bonis filiis hominum)*	—	—	partly	
„ 48	*dolentes et moerentes*	—	+	partly	
„ „	*ibamus et quaerebamus te*	—	—	—	
iv. 16	*in Bethsaida*	no name	o	—	note

Luke.	E_m	A_c	Sc.	Pesh.	
viii. 31	*in Gehennam* ...	—	+	—	
„ 47	*(hoc quoque ei absconditum non esse)* ...	—	+	—	
„ 50	*(firmiter crede)* ...	—	+	—	
x. 1	*juxta* vel *ad similitudinem suam*	—	—	—	
„ 39	*venit M. et sedit* ...	+	+	+	
„ 40	*non est tibi cura de me* ...	—	+	—	
„ 42	*ut in aeternum ab ea non auferatur* ...	—	—	—	
xi. 52	*claves* ...	+	+	—	
xii. 42	*quis erit procurator, servus fidelis, beneficus et sapiens ?*	partly	+	—	
xv. 32	*vivit et ad vitam revocatus est*	—	o	—	
xvi. 25	*cruciatus suos* ...	—	o	—	
xix. 5	*descende instinc* ...	—	—	—	
„ 8	*omnia quae unquam ab aliquo injuste accepi* ...	—	partly	partly	
„ 39	*homines* ...	—	partly	—	
„ 42	*si cognovisses tu saltem hunc diem pacis tuae sed abscondita est pax a facie tua*	—	+	—	
xx. 34	*filii adulti* ...	—	—	—	
xxii. 21	*manus . . . . mecum in mensa extensa est* ...	—	—	—	
„ 32	*oravi Patrem pro te* ...	—	—	—	
„ 36	*gladium suum* ...	—	—	—	
„ 38	*sufficiunt duo* ...	+	+	+	
xxiii. 39	*nonne tu es Christus ille ?* ...	—	+	—	
„ „	*et nos tecum* ...	+	+	+	
„ 43	*in horto voluptatis* ...	—	partly	—	
„ 48	*vae fuit, vae fuit nobis, filius Dei erat hic* ...	—	partly	—	see note
„ 49	*cognati Jesu* ...	—	—	—	

Passing by the controversy about the date and origin of the Curetonian Syriac, with which I am not competent to deal, I now proceed to give a few examples of the kind of text found in the Arabic Harmony.

PASSAGES WHICH RESEMBLE THE PESHITTO.

M. xi. 22.　Tyre and Sidon will have rest in the day of judgment.

M. xxii. 19.　the penny of the census.

Mar. ix. 29.   except by fasting and prayer.

Mar. x. 46.   Timaeus the son of Timaeus.

L. ix. 31.   And they thought that the time of his future advent which was to be accomplished in Jerusalem had now come.   But Simon and they that were with him had been heavy with sleep, and were hardly awaked when they saw his glory, and the two men who were standing near him.   And when these had begun to depart from him, Simon says to Jesus, Teacher, it is good that we should be here . . . and when they had seen Moses and Elias entering into the cloud they were afraid again.

L. xvii. 7.   leading oxen or feeding sheep.

L. xviii. 14.   rather than that Pharisee.

PASSAGES WHICH DIFFER FROM THE PESHITTO.

M. xii. 24.   Beelzebub, the prince of the demons, who is in him.

M. xiii. 55.   Is not this the carpenter, the son of the carpenter ? (*Conflate.*)

M. xvi. 22.   But Simon Cephas as if pitying him.

M. xvii. 26.   Give thou also to them as if thou wert a stranger.

M. xxiii. 24.   straining out a gnat but ornamenting a camel.

Mar. vii. 26.   of Hemesen of Syria.

L. xix. 22.   servant worthless, negligent, unfaithful.

L. xix. 28.   Jesus went forward at a gentle gait.

J. v. 2.   Betharrahmat.

J. vii. 5.   For up to this time neither did the brethren of Jesus believe in him.

J. xix. 17.   But the Jews took Jesus.

www.ingramcontent.com/pod-product-compliance
Lightning Source LLC
Chambersburg PA
CBHW032144010726
47493CB00008BA/2578